THE
VEGETARIAN
SLOW COOKER

Joanna White

BRISTOL PUBLISHING ENTERPRISES
Hayward, California

A nitty gritty® Cookbook

Printed in the United States of America.

ISBN: 1-55867-268-0

Cover design: Frank J. Paredes
Cover photography: John A. Benson
Food stylist: Susan Devaty
Illustrator: Hannah Suhr

CONTENTS

VEGETARIAN SLOW COOKING

The slow cooker is a marvelous kitchen convenience that has been popular since it was first introduced in the 1960s. But while the slow cooker has stayed very much the same, what we know about diet has undergone great change in the last 40 years. For reasons of health, or conviction, or just because meatless foods are delicious enough to satisfy, people are eating less meat, or no longer eat meat.

It is a delight to put recipes together early in the morning, and come home to a ready meal. Because so many of you want foods that are both vegetarian and can be made in this favorite appliance, this book has been created to provide you with an abundant resource of slow-cooking meatless recipes. In addition, the appendix contains information about alternatives to meat and dairy products that you can purchase or make yourself.

GOOD THINGS TO KNOW

- There are generally two slow cooker settings: low (200°) and high (300°). Low is recommended for slow, "all-day" cooking. One hour on high heat is equivalent to about two to two hours thirty minutes on low heat.

- Beans should be softened completely before combining with sugar or acid foods. These foods have a tendency to harden beans and will prevent softening. Discard water after soaking or boiling.

- Use whole-leaf herbs and spices for all-day cooking. Ground herbs and spices should be stirred in during the last hour of cooking.

- Avoid stirring food in the slow cooker when cooking on low heat because removing the cover releases too much heat. Stirring occasionally on high heat will help to distribute the flavor. Never remove the lid during the first 2 hours of baking.

- Dairy products like milk, sweet and sour cream and cheeses have a tendency to break down during long hours of cooking. Add dairy products just before serving or substitute undiluted condensed soups or evaporated milk.

- Rice and pasta have a tendency to become mushy after long hours of cooking. Either add raw rice or pasta during the last hour of cooking or stir in precooked starches just before serving.

- If your recipe ends up with too much liquid, take off the lid and cook on high heat for 45 minutes.

- If you are worried about not being able to return in time to unplug your slow cooker, consider investing in an automatic timer. However, hot food should not be left out for more than 2 hours.

- The slow cooker should always be at least half-filled for best results.
- Liquids should generally be added last.
- Certain foods need to have a brown color: in this case, simply place cooked vegetables or dessert under a broiler for several minutes to brown and crisp the food before serving.
- The higher the setting, the more liquid required.
- Always allow more time when cooking at higher altitudes.
- Always bake on the high temperature setting: otherwise dough will not rise properly and will become gummy.
- Root vegetables like carrots, turnips, parsnips and rutabagas, quite often take longer to cook than the meat. It is best to layer these on the bottom of the cooker and let the liquid keep the vegetables moist (which helps them cook more evenly).

ADAPTING RECIPES

Reduce liquid to about half the recommended amount.

The flavor of leaf or whole herbs and spices may increase with cooking, so start out using $\frac{1}{2}$ the amount called for in your regular recipe. Taste about 1 hour before serving and add more herbs and spices at this time if necessary.

Soup recipes can often require two to three quarts of water. In slow cookers, it is better to add all the other ingredients first and then add only enough water to cover. If you wish a thinner soup, add more water at the end of cooking.

If milk-based recipes have no other liquid for initial cooking, cook with one to two cups of water, and then stir in milk or cream just before serving.

Remember that in slow cooking the liquids do not "boil away": generally, you will end up with more liquid at the end of cooking.

Baking usually requires placing the ingredients in a separate container (like a coffee can or a steam pudding mold). Cover the can with foil; tie down the foil with string and surround can with one to two cups hot water.

TIME GUIDE

IF RECIPE SAYS COOK:	COOK TIME IN SLOW COOKER
15 to 20 minutes	1 ½ to 2 hours on high heat *or* 4 to 6 hours on low heat
35 to 45 minutes	3 to 4 hours on high heat *or* 6 to 10 hours on low heat
50 minutes to 3 hours	4 to 6 hours on high heat *or* 8 to 18 hours on low heat

MAIN DISHES

LASAGNA

This is a delicious dish that would go well with a crisp salad, garlic bread and a fruit dessert. Fresh noodles or oven-ready lasagna noodles require no precooking. For a change, try using fresh spinach noodles in this recipe.

1 small eggplant
$1/2$ tsp. salt
2 tbs. olive oil, divided
$1/3$ lb. mushrooms (prefer shiitake)
2 small leeks
1 tbs. butter
$2^1/2$ cups commercially prepared tomato sauce or *Basil Tomato Sauce*, page 10
8 oz. oven-ready or fresh lasagna noodles
1 cup grated Parmesan cheese, divided
2 cups ricotta cheese
$1^1/2$ cups grated Monterey Jack cheese
1 medium zucchini, peeled and cut into $1/8$-inch-thick slices

Cut eggplant into $1/2$-inch rounds. Lay slices on a towel and sprinkle with salt. Allow eggplant to stand for 30 minutes. This will remove bitterness. Rinse slices with cold water and pat dry with paper towels. Place slices on a baking sheet and brush with 1 tbs. olive oil. Heat broiler, broil both sides of eggplant until brown and set aside.

Cut mushrooms into $1/4$-inch-thick slices. Remove tough green tops from leeks and cut each leek in half. Thoroughly clean dirt between leaves and cut into $1/2$-inch slices.

In a skillet, melt butter with remaining 1 tbs. olive oil. Sauté mushrooms and leeks for about 5 to 8 minutes, until wilted. Stir in tomato sauce and set aside.

In a bowl, combine $1/2$ cup Parmesan cheese, ricotta cheese and Monterey Jack cheese.

To assemble, spread $1/3$ of the tomato vegetable sauce on the bottom of the slow cooker. Cover with a layer of lasagna noodles. Spread $1/3$ of the cheese mixture over noodles and layer with eggplant slices. Cover with more noodles and another layer of sauce. Again layer with noodles, spread with another $1/3$ of the cheese mixture and cover with zucchini slices. Top with noodles and remaining sauce. Finish with remaining cheese mixture and sprinkle top with remaining $1/2$ cup Parmesan cheese. Cook on low heat for 4 to 6 hours.

MIXED NUT LOAF

This is a delicious alternative to meat loaf, especially when served with Onion Gravy, *page 9. I have also used this mixture as a filling to stuff mushrooms for an appetizer. Simply stir in 1 cup frozen spinach that has been thawed and squeezed dry, fill mushrooms with mixture and bake for 1 hour at 350.°*

2–3 tbs. olive oil
3 medium onions, chopped
2½ cups chopped celery
¾ cup chopped walnuts
¾ cup pecans or sunflower seeds,
  ground into a meal

2–2½ cups milk
1½ tsp. salt
1½ tsp. dried basil
½ tsp. sage, or more to taste
1 pinch pepper, optional
3 cups fresh breadcrumbs

Heat olive oil on medium-high heat in a skillet. Sauté onions and celery for about 5 minutes, until tender. Stir in remaining ingredients, taste and adjust seasonings. Lightly oil the slow cooker and pour mixture in. Cook on low heat for 6 to 8 hours, or on high heat for 3 to 4 hours.

ONION GRAVY

Carrots can be substituted for onions in this recipe. You can make this gravy on the stove, but if you prefer to use the slow cooker, substitute flour for corn-starch and cook on high heat for 1 to 2 hours. Serve this alongside Mixed Nut Loaf, page 8.

1 tbs. olive oil
½ cup diced onion or carrots
3 tbs. soy sauce, or more to taste
3 tbs. cornstarch
2 cups boiling water
pepper to taste

Heat olive oil on medium-high in a saucepan and sauté onion until soft. Mix soy sauce with cornstarch and stir into boiling water until mixture thickens. Stir in onions and pepper, if desired. Taste and add more soy sauce if desired.

BASIL TOMATO SAUCE

Makes 2½ cups

If you prefer to use fresh tomatoes, substitute 2 lb. ripe (preferably plum) tomatoes for canned tomatoes. Always deseed tomatoes before chopping and use fresh basil when available.

2 tbs. olive oil
¾ cup chopped onions
1½ tsp. minced garlic
1 can (28 oz.) whole plum tomatoes, drained
¼ cup chopped fresh parsley, or 4 tsp. dried

3–4 tbs. chopped fresh basil, or 1 tbs. dried
1 tbs. chopped fresh oregano, or 1 tsp. dried
1 tbs. sugar
1 tsp. salt
½ tsp. pepper

Heat olive oil in a skillet on medium-high heat and sauté onions for about 4 to 5 minutes, until wilted. Add garlic and sauté for 1 minute. Dice drained tomatoes (reserve drained juice to thin sauce if desired). Stir in tomatoes, onions, fresh herbs and spices and simmer for 20 minutes. Taste and adjust seasonings. If you wish to use the slow cooker for this sauce, cook on low heat for 1½ hours.

LENTILS WITH ALMONDS AND RAISINS

This dish can be served by itself, over rice or on baked potatoes. The seasonings in this recipe tend towards a Spanish influence, but the spices can easily be changed to curry or Italian seasonings for variety. Try cranberry sauce or Cranberry Chutney, *page 106, with this dish.*

1 tbs. olive oil
1 cup lentils
1 tsp. cinnamon
1 tsp. ground cardamom
1 bay leaf
3 cups *Vegetable Broth,* page 48
1/2 cup raisins or dried currants

1/4 cup chopped toasted almonds or
   pumpkin seeds
1/2 cup plain yogurt or sour cream
1/2 tsp. ground cumin
1/8–1/4 tsp. cayenne pepper
black pepper to taste

In a skillet, heat oil on medium-high heat and stir-fry lentils for 2 to 3 minutes. Transfer toasted lentils to the slow cooker with cinnamon, cardamom, bay leaf and vegetable broth. Cook on low heat for 9 to 10 hours or until lentils are tender. Set slow cooker on high and stir in raisins and almonds. In a small bowl, mix yogurt with cumin, cayenne and black pepper. Stir in yogurt mixture and heat until warm. Remove bay leaf before serving. Taste and adjust seasonings before serving.

EGGPLANT PARMESAN CASSEROLE

This dish consists of layers of eggplant, tomato sauce and cheese. Browning the eggplant really adds to the flavor and texture. Serve this with a crunchy salad, glazed carrots and a simple fruit dessert.

1 medium eggplant
1/4 cup olive oil, divided
salt and pepper to taste
1 medium onion, diced
1 tsp. minced garlic
3 medium tomatoes, peeled, seeded and chopped
1/2 tsp. sugar
1 tsp. dried basil
3/4 cup ricotta cheese
1 egg
2/3 cup freshly grated Parmesan cheese, divided
1/2 cup heavy cream or nut cream
1 tbs. minced fresh parsley
1/8 tsp. nutmeg
1 pinch ground allspice

Cut eggplant lengthwise into ³/₄-inch slices and place on a baking sheet. Brush slices with olive oil on both sides and sprinkle with salt and pepper. Place under a broiler and cook until eggplant is softened and browned on both sides. Set aside.

In a skillet on medium-high heat, sauté onion and garlic in remaining olive oil until onion is translucent. Add tomatoes, sugar, basil, salt and pepper and cook for 15 minutes or until most of the liquid has evaporated.

Combine ricotta, egg, ¹/₂ of the Parmesan, cream, parsley, nutmeg, allspice and salt in a bowl. Place a layer of eggplant in the slow cooker, cover with ¹/₂ of the tomato sauce and layer remaining eggplant over sauce. Pour remaining tomato sauce over top layer of eggplant, spoon on ricotta mixture and sprinkle with remaining Parmesan cheese. Cover and cook on low heat for 5 to 6 hours.

MANY BEAN CHILI

This colorful chili would go well with cornbread, served in a hollowed-out bread bowl. If you wish to make a faster version, use 1 can (15 oz.) beans for each ³/₄ cup dried beans to avoid the bean rehydrating process.

³/₄ cup dried kidney beans
³/₄ cup dried black beans
³/₄ cup dried pinto beans
6–8 cups water
2 tbs. olive oil
2 medium onions, diced
2 tsp. minced garlic
1 red bell pepper, cut into ¹/₂-inch squares
1 green bell pepper, cut into ¹/₂-inch squares
1 can (4 oz.) diced green chiles

1 jalapeño chile, finely diced, optional
1 bunch fresh parsley, finely chopped
1 can (28 oz.) chopped tomatoes with juice
4 tsp. salt
1 tsp. ground cumin
1 tsp. dried oregano
2 tbs. chili powder
1 bay leaf
2 cups water
3 tbs. chopped fresh cilantro

Place kidney beans, black beans and pinto beans in the slow cooker with water and soak overnight. Cook on high heat for 2 to 3 hours until beans are just tender. Drain off any excess water.

Heat olive oil in a skillet on medium-high heat and sauté onions for 5 minutes. Add garlic, bell peppers and green chiles and cook for 2 more minutes. Transfer this mixture to slow cooker, along with parsley, tomatoes, salt, cumin, oregano, chili powder, bay leaf and water. Cook on low heat for 8 to 9 hours, or on high heat for 4 to 4$\frac{1}{2}$ hours.

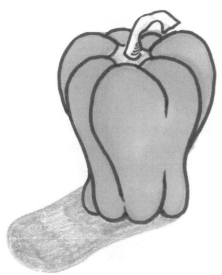

Remove bay leaf before serving. Just before serving, add cilantro. Taste and adjust seasonings. If you prefer a thinner chili, add more water or additional chopped tomatoes.

CONFETTI RICE AND VEGETABLES

This colorful dish would go well with crunchy coleslaw or a green salad. The addition of Parmesan cheese really adds a new dimension of flavor.

2 tbs. butter
2 tbs. olive oil
2 cups long-grain rice
3/4 cup chopped onion
1 tsp. minced garlic
1 red bell pepper, cut into 2-inch pieces
1 cup 2-inch green bean pieces
1 cup chopped carrots
1 1/2 cups *Vegetable Broth,* page 48
1 can (8 oz.) tomato sauce

1 can (16 oz.) chopped tomatoes with juice
1 tsp. Italian seasoning
1 tsp. sugar
1 tsp. salt
1/2 tsp. dried oregano
1/2 tsp. dried rosemary, crushed
1/4 tsp. Tabasco Sauce
freshly ground black pepper to taste
3/4–1 cup grated Parmesan cheese

In a skillet, heat $1/2$ of the butter and olive oil on medium-high heat and sauté rice until golden brown. Pour browned rice into the slow cooker.

Heat remaining butter and oil in skillet and sauté onions for about 5 minutes, until wilted. Add cooked onions to slow cooker with garlic, bell peppers, green beans, carrots, vegetable broth, tomato sauce, tomatoes, Italian seasoning, sugar, salt, oregano, rosemary and Tabasco. Stir well, cover and cook on low heat for 4 to 6 hours, or on high heat for 2 to 3 hours.

Serve with a sprinkling of freshly grated pepper and grated Parmesan cheese.

PICADILLO SWEET BEANS

This fast recipe can be served over cornbread, couscous or sweet potatoes. Black beans, pinto beans or garbanzos can be substituted for kidney beans. You can substitute 1¹/₂ cups dried beans for canned beans; simply cover with water, cook on high heat for 2 hours, add remaining ingredients and cook on low heat for 8 to 9 hours. A cucumber salad would be a good accompaniment for this dish.

2 tbs. butter
1 large red bell pepper, diced
1 large green bell pepper, diced
1 medium onion, chopped
1 tsp. minced garlic
¹/₂ cup tomato sauce

2 cans (15 oz. each) kidney beans with
   liquid
¹/₄–¹/₂ cup raisins
1 tbs. ground cumin
¹/₄ tsp. cayenne pepper

In a skillet on medium-high, melt butter and sauté peppers, onion and garlic for about 5 minutes or until onion is soft.

Transfer pepper mixture to the slow cooker with tomato sauce, kidney beans, raisins, cumin and cayenne. Cover and cook on low heat for 6 to 8 hours. Taste and adjust seasonings.

RUTABAGA AND POTATO CASSEROLE

This specialty dish from Finland has a slightly sweet flavor. Serve with a crisp salad, colorful steamed vegetables and a fruit dessert. Do not use a food processor to mash the vegetables in this recipe, as they will become gluey.

1 lb. new potatoes, peeled and cut into
   1-inch cubes
3/4 lb. rutabagas, peeled and cut into
   1-inch cubes
cold water to cover vegetables
2/3 cup cream
1/3 cup fine dry breadcrumbs

2 large eggs, beaten
1 1/2 tbs. dark corn syrup
1 tsp. salt
1/4 tsp. nutmeg
white pepper to taste, optional
2 tbs. butter, melted

Place potatoes and rutabagas in the slow cooker and cover with water to 1 inch. Cover and cook on high heat for 2 to 4 hours or until vegetables are tender. Drain vegetables in a colander and, while still warm, force through a ricer, food mill or sieve. Mix cream, breadcrumbs and remaining ingredients together. Stir mixture into mashed vegetables and return to slow cooker. Cover and cook on high heat for 1 hour or low heat for 2 to 2 1/2 hours. If desired, spoon mixture into an ovenproof dish and place under broiler until top is slightly brown.

WHITE BEAN STEW

This is a wonderful vegetable stew made from Great Northern beans and parsnips. The bell peppers are added at the last minute to give color. Serve with steamed green vegetables and a colorful fruit salad.

2 cups dried great Northern beans
   (white beans)
2 qt. water
1 tsp. salt
1 bay leaf
1 1/2 tsp. dried thyme, divided
1 lb. shallots, cut in half

1 lb. parsnips, peeled and cut into
   2-inch pieces
1 tsp. sugar
2 tbs. butter
2 large red bell peppers, halved
salt and pepper to taste

Place beans in the slow cooker with water, salt, bay leaf and 1 tsp. of the thyme. Cover and cook on high heat for 2 hours. Add remaining thyme, shallots, parsnips, sugar and butter. Cover and cook on low heat for 7 to 9 hours or until parsnips are tender. Deseed red peppers and place on a baking sheet, cut-side down. Place under the broiler and allow skins to char black. Remove peppers from oven and place in a brown paper bag for 10 minutes. Peel and coarsely chop peppers. Stir into bean stew and add salt and pepper. Taste and adjust seasonings. Remove bay leaf before serving.

BULGUR PILAF WITH GARBANZO BEANS

Bulgur is also called cracked wheat and can be found in most health food stores or large supermarkets. If fresh dill is available, use 2 tbs. finely chopped, in place of dried dill.

2 tbs. olive oil
1 large onion, diced
2 tsp. minced garlic
2 cups bulgur wheat
2½ cups water
1 can (15 oz.) garbanzo beans, rinsed
   and drained

¾ cup diced sun-dried tomatoes
salt and pepper to taste
¼ cup chopped fresh parsley or
   cilantro
1½ tbs. fresh lemon juice, or more to
   taste
1–2 tsp. dried dill weed

In a skillet on medium-high heat, heat olive oil and sauté onion for about 3 to 5 minutes, until soft. Add garlic and sauté for 1 minute. Transfer onion mixture to the slow cooker. Add bulgur, water, garbanzo and sun-dried tomatoes. Cover and cook on low heat for 8 to 9 hours. Add salt, pepper, parsley, lemon juice and dill weed. Taste and adjust seasonings.

CASHEW AND RICE LOAF

Servings: 6

This high-protein dish can have many variations, such as almonds instead of cashews, sesame seeds or chopped pumpkin seeds instead of sunflower seeds and white rice instead of brown. Try this with a Caesar salad, steamed seasoned carrots and berry crisp for dessert.

1 cup toasted cashew nuts
1/2 cup sunflower seeds
3/4 cup chopped onions
1 cup milk
2 1/2 cups cooked brown rice
1/2 cup wheat germ

1/4 cup chopped fresh parsley
2 tsp. vegetable bouillon granules
1 tsp. onion salt, or to taste
1 tsp. dried basil
1/2 tsp. Italian seasoning

With a blender or food processor, pulse to blend together cashews, sunflower seeds, onions and milk. Pour into a bowl and stir in remaining ingredients. Taste and adjust seasonings. Grease the slow cooker, add rice mixture, cover and cook on low heat for 4 to 6 hours.

CARROT NUT LOAF

The unusual ingredient in this recipe is peanuts. A good accompaniment would be Caponata, *page 66, or* Red Cabbage With Fruit and Onions, *page 69, and a crunchy green salad.*

2 tbs. peanut oil	2 cups grated sharp cheddar cheese
1 cup chopped onions	3 cups milk
1 cup chopped celery	4 large eggs
2 cups diced cooked carrots	1–2 tsp. salt
1 cup finely chopped peanuts	1/3 cup peanut butter
1 pkg (8 oz.) cornbread stuffing mix	2 cups warm water

Heat oil in a skillet on medium-high heat and sauté onions and celery for about 5 minutes, until soft. Transfer mixture to the slow cooker with carrots, peanuts, stuffing mix and cheddar cheese.

In a bowl, mix together milk, eggs, salt and peanut butter. Stir into carrot mixture.

Press mixture into a buttered baking dish, cover with foil and tie with string. Place baking dish on a trivet or rack in the slow cooker and add 2 cups warm water. Cover and cook on low heat for 6 to 8 hours.

MEXICAN BEAN POT

This flavorful bean dish is spiced with oregano and sweetened with molasses. Serve with a rice side dish, a tossed salad with vinaigrette dressing and key lime pie for dessert.

1 lb. dried navy or white beans
1 qt. water
1 1/2 cups chopped onions
3 tbs. olive oil
2 large green bell peppers
1 can (1 lb.) diced tomatoes with juice
1/2 cup dark molasses

2 tsp. dried oregano
2 tsp. salt, or to taste
1/2 tsp. cumin seeds, crushed
1/2 tsp. black pepper
1/2 tsp. minced garlic
1 dash Tabasco Sauce
1/2 cup brown or maple sugar, optional

Soak beans in water overnight. Cover and cook beans and onions in the slow cooker on high heat for 2 to 3 hours. Beans should be tender, not mushy.

In a skillet, heat oil on medium-high heat and sauté bell peppers until soft. Transfer peppers to slow cooker with remaining ingredients. Add sugar if you prefer sweeter beans. Cover and cook on low heat for 7 to 9 hours. Taste and adjust seasonings.

VEGETABLE STEW

A large (28 oz.) can of tomatoes can be substituted for fresh tomatoes in this recipe. Serve with cheese, a crisp tossed salad and crusty bread.

1/4 cup olive oil, divided
1 cup chopped onions
2 small zucchini, sliced
1 medium green bell pepper, sliced
1 tsp. minced garlic
1 medium eggplant, peeled and cut
  into strips
1/4 cup flour
4 tomatoes, peeled, seeded and cut
  into large dice

1/4 cup ketchup
1 bay leaf
1 tbs. salt
1 tsp. cider vinegar
1/2 tsp. dried oregano
1/4 tsp. black pepper
1/2 tsp. dried basil, optional
1 cup *Vegetable Broth*, page 48,
  optional

In a skillet on medium-high heat, heat 3 tbs. of the oil and sauté onions, zucchini, bell pepper and garlic until onions are translucent. Transfer to the slow cooker. Coat eggplant strips in flour, add remaining oil to skillet and cook eggplant strips to a light brown. Add strips to slow cooker. Add remaining ingredients, except vegetable broth. Cover and cook on high heat for 3 to 4 hours. Taste and adjust seasonings. Remove bay leaf before serving. If you wish more moisture, add vegetable broth.

CHILI CORN PIE

This is a vegetarian chili loaded with beans and corn and covered with a cheesy cornmeal topping. If you wish to add more protein, add crumbled firm tofu. If you like your chili hot, increase the amount of chili powder or use a hotter variety of chili powder.

2 tbs. vegetable oil
1 red bell pepper, seeded and diced
1 green bell pepper, seeded and diced
1 large stalk celery, diced
1 tsp. minced garlic
1 tsp. hot or regular chili powder, to taste
1 can (14 oz.) chopped tomatoes with juice
1 can (11 oz.) corn, drained, or 2 cups frozen corn
1 can (7 oz.) kidney beans, rinsed and drained

$1/4$ cup chopped fresh cilantro leaves
salt to taste, optional
$2/3$ cup cornmeal
1 tbs. flour
$1/2$ tsp. salt
1 tbs. baking powder
1 tbs. sugar
1 large egg, beaten
6 tbs. milk
4 tsp. vegetable oil
1 cup grated sharp cheddar cheese

In a skillet on medium-high heat, heat oil and sauté bell peppers and celery for several minutes, until vegetables become soft. Add garlic and cook for 1 minute. Transfer to the slow cooker. Add chili powder, tomatoes, corn, kidney beans and cilantro. Stir mixture, taste and add salt if desired. Cover and cook on high heat for 3 hours.

In a bowl, combine cornmeal, flour, salt and sugar and make a well in the center. Place egg, milk and oil in well and incorporate into flour mixture until a smooth batter is formed. Drop dough onto bean and corn mixture, leaving a 1/2-inch space around the edge to allow steam to escape. Cover and cook for 30 minutes on high heat or until dough is cooked. Note: Do not lift lid or dough will become soggy. Sprinkle with cheese, cover and cook for 5 to 10 minutes to allow cheese to melt.

VEGETABLE CURRY

Servings: 4

A typical Indian meal consists of a curry main dish, basmati rice, fresh tomato chutney, yogurt flavored with some herb or spice, and naan flat bread. If you like your curry hot, add the entire red chile pepper. Ginger also adds "heat" to a recipe.

2 tbs. vegetable oil
1 cup sliced onion
1 1/2 tbs. ground coriander
2 tsp. cumin seeds
2 tsp. ground ginger, or to taste
1 tsp. minced garlic
1 tsp. turmeric
1 tsp. chopped red chile pepper, optional
1 can (14 oz.) chopped tomatoes with juice
1 1/3 cups coconut milk

1 small cauliflower
2 small zucchini, sliced
2 carrots, sliced
2 boiling potatoes, diced
1 can (14 oz.) garbanzo beans, rinsed and drained
3/4–1 cup plain yogurt
3 tbs. mango chutney
1/4 cup chopped fresh cilantro leaves
salt and pepper to taste
finely diced red bell pepper and cilantro leaves for garnish

In a skillet on medium-high heat, heat oil and sauté onion for about 4 to 5 minutes, until wilted. Add coriander, cumin, ginger, garlic, turmeric and chile pepper. Sauté for 1 minute to bring out flavor of spices.

Transfer to the slow cooker. Add tomatoes and coconut milk and stir to combine. Break cauliflower into florets and add to cooker. Add zucchini, carrots, potatoes and garbanzo beans. Stir to combine. Cover and cook on high heat for 3 to 4 hours, or on low heat for 6 to 9 hours.

Before serving, add yogurt, chutney, cilantro, salt and pepper. Taste and adjust seasonings. Garnish curry with finely diced red pepper and cilantro leaves for color.

ITALIAN EGGPLANT AND BEANS

Servings: 8

This dish goes well with cumin rice with nuts, ultimate wild rice or stuffed potatoes. A crisp tossed salad is a must and maybe a light lemon or lime mousse for dessert.

1 lb. dried kidney beans
5 cups water, divided
2–3 tbs. olive oil
1 cup chopped onions
1 small eggplant
1 can (1 lb.) diced tomatoes

2 tsp. salt
1 tsp. dried marjoram
$\frac{1}{2}$ tsp. dried basil
$\frac{1}{2}$ cup dry red wine
2 tsp. sugar
pepper to taste, optional

Soak beans overnight in 4 cups of the water. Cover and cook beans in the slow cooker for 2 hours on high heat. Drain beans in a colander and return to slow cooker.

Heat oil in a skillet on medium-high heat and sauté onions for 2 to 3 minutes. Cut eggplant into large dice, add to skillet and cook for 2 minutes. Transfer to slow cooker. Add tomato, salt, marjoram, basil, wine, sugar and pepper. Cover and cook on low heat for 8 to 10 hours. Taste and adjust seasonings before serving.

MUSHROOM AND PARMESAN RICE

For the best flavor, always use freshly grated Parmesan cheese. To vary the flavors, try using different types of mushrooms.

2 tbs. olive oil
1 1/4 cups long-grain rice
1 tsp. minced garlic
1 cup chopped onions
2 stalks celery, chopped
1 red or green bell pepper, seeded and
  chopped
1/2 lb. mushrooms, sliced

1 tsp. lemon juice
1/2 tsp. dried oregano
1/2 tsp. dried basil
4 cups *Vegetable Broth*, page 48
1/4–1/2 cup diced sun-dried tomatoes
3/4 cup freshly grated Parmesan cheese
salt and pepper to taste

In a large skillet on medium-high heat, heat oil and sauté rice for 5 minutes, until rice begins to brown. Add garlic, onions, celery and bell peppers and cook until soft. Add mushrooms and lemon juice to skillet and cook for 2 minutes.

Transfer to the slow cooker. Add oregano, basil and vegetable broth. Cover and cook on high heat for 2 to 3 hours, or on low heat for 6 to 8 hours. Gently stir in sun-dried tomatoes and Parmesan cheese. Taste and add salt and pepper if desired.

GREEK EGGPLANT MOUSSAKA

Servings: 6

Traditionally, moussaka is made with ground lamb and layered with a béchamel (white) sauce. Here, eggplant replaces the lamb. Serve with a Greek salad and bread. It is actually better to make this recipe the day before so the flavors can meld.

1 $3/4$ lb. eggplant, unpeeled
1 tbs. salt
$1/4$ cup olive oil
2 tbs. butter
3 tbs. flour
1 $3/4$ cups *Vegetable Broth*, page 48, warmed
$1/2$ tsp. salt
$1/4$ tsp. white pepper

1 large pinch nutmeg
2 large eggs
2–3 tsp. cinnamon
1 cup ricotta cheese
1 $1/2$ cups grated Parmesan cheese
$1/4$ cup chopped fresh parsley
cayenne pepper to taste
1 $1/2$ cups canned tomato sauce, prefer basil flavor

Cut eggplant into ¼-inch-thick slices. Place slices on paper towels and sprinkle with salt. After 30 minutes, rinse slices in cold water and pat dry. This will help remove any bitter flavor. Brush cookie sheet and eggplant slices with olive oil and broil, turning, until brown on each side.

In a saucepan on medium heat, melt butter, stir in flour to form a roux and cook for 1 minute. Gradually stir in warmed vegetable broth and season with salt, white pepper and nutmeg. Remove from heat. Stir in eggs, cinnamon, ricotta, 1 cup of the Parmesan, parsley and cayenne to taste. Stir until smooth.

Pour ⅓ of the tomato sauce into the slow cooker. Cover with ⅓ of the ricotta sauce and ⅓ of the eggplant slices. Sprinkle with 2 tbs. Parmesan cheese. Repeat these steps to use all ingredients. Cover and cook on low heat for 6 to 8 hours.

RICE GUMBO

Serve this stew over rice. Kohlrabi is a crisp vegetable that may be hard to acquire. Use jicama, water chestnuts or Jerusalem artichokes if kohlrabi is unavailable.

4 large tomatoes
2 medium red bell peppers
1/4 cup olive oil
1 cup diced onions
2 stalks celery, diced
1 green bell pepper, diced
1/4 cup flour
2 cups *Vegetable Broth,* page 48
1 tsp. dried thyme
1 tsp. dried oregano
1 pinch dried basil
2 cups canned black-eyed peas
3 small kohlrabi, peeled and cut into
   2-inch pieces
4 carrots, cut into 2-inch pieces

1 small head broccoli, stem removed,
   separated into 2-inch florets
6 okra, ends trimmed and cut into
   2-inch pieces
2 small zucchini, unpeeled, cut into
   2-inch pieces
1 cup frozen corn
salt and pepper to taste
5 cups water
2 1/2 cups long-grain rice
2–3 tsp. salt
1 tsp. lemon juice
3 tbs. butter
1/2 cup chopped fresh parsley or cilantro
2 1/2 tsp. dried thyme
1 tsp. paprika

Cut tomatoes in half and squeeze out excess seeds. Cut red bell pepper in half and remove seeds. Place tomatoes and peppers cut-side down on a baking sheet and place under the broiler. Broil until skins just begin to char. Chop slightly charred vegetables into a coarse dice and set aside.

In a large skillet on medium-high heat, heat oil and cook onions, celery and green peppers for about 5 to 6 minutes, until slightly brown. Stir in flour and continue stirring until flour begins to brown. Add vegetable broth, thyme, oregano and basil and stir to combine. Pour mixture into the slow cooker with black-eyed peas, kohlrabi, carrots, broccoli and okra. Cover and cook on low heat for 7 to 9 hours, or on high heat for 3 to 4 hours. Add zucchini and corn and cook on low heat for 1 hour. Taste and determine if you wish to add salt and pepper. Serve over rice.

To cook rice: Bring water to boil in a medium saucepan and add rice, salt and lemon juice. Reduce heat to a simmer and cook for 15 to 18 minutes. Stir in butter, parsley, thyme and paprika. Taste and adjust seasonings.

JAMBALAYA

Servings: 8

This is a vegetarian adaptation of the classic Creole dish. If you desire a closer version, fry pieces of soy sausage or add cooked prawns. Serve on rice and top with chopped parsley and chopped green onions. Serve grated cheddar cheese alongside.

2 tbs. olive oil
2 tbs. butter
1 cup chopped onions
1 tsp. minced garlic
3 bay leaves
1 1/4 cups sliced carrots
1 cup chopped celery
3/4 cup coarsely chopped red bell peppers
3/4 cup coarsely chopped green bell peppers
2 1/2 tsp. dried basil

1/2 tsp. dried thyme
2 cups chopped tomatoes, canned or fresh
1 pkg. (10 oz.) frozen okra, or 1 can (15 oz.) baby corn, drained
3 cups *Vegetable Broth*, page 48
2 tbs. finely chopped fresh parsley
1/4 tsp. cayenne pepper, or to taste
1/8 tsp. ground allspice
salt and black pepper to taste
1/4 cup olive oil
1/3 cup flour

In a skillet on medium-high heat, heat oil and butter and sauté onions for 5 minutes. Add garlic and cook for 1 minute. Transfer to the slow cooker. Add bay leaves, carrots, celery, peppers, basil, thyme, tomatoes, okra, vegetable broth, parsley, cayenne, allspice, salt and pepper. Cover and cook on low heat for 9 to 10 hours.

About 1 hour before serving, heat olive oil on medium-high in a small saucepan and add flour. Reduce heat to a simmer and cook until well browned, stirring frequently with a whisk. This will take about 30 minutes; be careful not to burn. Stir this into slow cooker and allow mixture to thicken for 30 minutes before serving. Taste and adjust seasonings. Serve over rice.

RICE CABBAGE ROLLS

This is a meatless version of a favorite family dish. Instead of hamburger and rice, this dish uses fresh vegetables and herbs with rice, rolled in cabbage and surrounded with a light, creamy tomato sauce. A good accompaniment would be Easy Scalloped Potatoes, *page 68.*

water for boiling
1 large green cabbage
1 tbs. butter
1 tbs. olive oil
1 large leek, cleaned and finely chopped, or 1 medium onion, chopped
1/2 cup chopped celery
1/2 cup finely chopped carrots
1 tsp. dried marjoram
1/2 tsp. dried thyme
salt and black pepper to taste
1 1/2 cups cooked white or brown rice
1/2 cup tomato juice
3 tomatoes, seeded and chopped
3/4 cup sour cream or plain yogurt

Prepare cabbage: Bring water to boil in a large stockpot. Cut deeply around core at base of cabbage, but do not try to remove it. Immerse entire cabbage in boiling water for 4 to 5 minutes. Remove from water and peel off 12 cabbage leaves. If leaves become difficult to remove, repeat the process to soften inner leaves. Remove tough stem from base of each leaf. With remaining cabbage, finely shred 1 cup cabbage to use in filling.

Heat butter and oil in a large skillet on medium-high heat. Sauté shredded cabbage, leek, celery and carrots for about 10 minutes, until vegetables begin to soften. Stir in marjoram, thyme, salt and pepper. Gently stir in rice. Taste and adjust seasonings.

Fill each cabbage with $1/12$ of the rice filling: Place a portion on the base of each leaf just above notched area, fold ends neatly around it, and roll. Use a toothpick to secure ends.

Place stuffed cabbage rolls seam-side down on a rack in the slow cooker. Pour tomato juice and chopped tomatoes over cabbage. Cover and cook on low heat for 5 to 7 hours. Transfer cabbage rolls to a serving platter. Stir sour cream into remaining juice and pour over rolls. Serve immediately.

SUPER VEGETARIAN CHILI

Servings: 8

This chili is made with pinto beans, vegetables and red wine. Serve this in a hollowed-out bread round with shredded cheddar cheese and chopped onions alongside.

1/2 cup dry red wine
1 cup chopped onions
1/2 cup finely chopped celery
1/4 cup finely diced green bell pepper
1 tbs. minced garlic
2/3 cup diced canned green chiles
3 cups chopped canned tomatoes
3 cups canned pinto beans, rinsed and drained

2 tbs. chopped fresh cilantro
1 tbs. chili powder
2 tsp. ground cumin
2 tsp. dried oregano
1 bay leaf
2 cups water
3 tbs. tomato paste
salt to taste

In a large saucepan on medium-high heat, heat wine, onions, celery, bell peppers and garlic together for 8 to 10 minutes.

Transfer to the slow cooker. Add all other ingredients except salt. Stir to combine. Cover and cook on low heat for 5 to 7 hours. Remove bay leaf before serving. Taste and add salt if desired.

BLACK BEAN NACHO SALAD

This salad is a variation of a favorite appetizer. Serve it with tortilla chips as a garnish.

1 lb. dried black beans
2 qt. cold water
1 tbs. salt
1 large onion, chopped
1 1/2 tsp. minced garlic
1 tbs. ground cumin
1 head lettuce, shredded

1 cup sliced black olives
1/2 cup diced green onions
1 1/2 cups chopped tomatoes
1 cup sour cream
diced avocados or guacamole, optional
tortilla chips for garnish

Place black beans in the slow cooker with cold water and soak overnight. Drain beans in a colander, rinse and add soaked beans back to slow cooker along with enough water to cover beans. Cover and cook on high heat for 2 to 3 hours, until beans are tender.

Add salt, onions, garlic and cumin, set slow cooker on low heat and cook for 8 hours. Taste and adjust seasonings.

Line individual serving plates with lettuce and top with cooked beans, olives, green onions, tomatoes and sour cream. Add avocados if desired, and garnish with tortilla chips.

MACARONI AND CASHEW CHEESE

If you prefer to use cheese, substitute 2 cups shredded cheddar or Monterey Jack cheese. The cheese should be added in the last half hour of cooking. You can substitute 2 tbs. chopped onion for onion salt, but you may need to increase salt to taste.

3 cups dried macaroni
1 cup raw cashews
2 tbs. raw sesame seeds
2 1/4 cups water, divided
1/4 cup canned pimientos, drained
1 tsp. onion salt

3/4 tsp. salt
1/2 tsp. minced garlic
2–3 tsp. lemon juice
1/8 tsp. celery seed
1/4 cup nutritional yeast, optional

Cook macaroni in salt water according to package instructions; rinse, drain and place in the slow cooker. With a blender, blend cashews, sesame seeds and 1 cup water for about 1 to 2 minutes, until mixture is creamy. Add remaining water and remaining ingredients and blend until smooth. Pour mixture into slow cooker and stir. Cook on high heat for 1 hour or on low heat for 2 to 3 hours.

SOUPS

BEET AND POTATO BORSCHT

Serve this with a dollop of sour cream on top or stirred into the soup.

1 tbs. olive oil
1 tbs. butter
1 cup diced onions
1 tsp. minced garlic
3 cups sliced red cabbage
3 small beets, peeled and cut into strips
3 boiling potatoes, in 3/4-inch chunks
2 cups chopped tomatoes
3 cups water or *Vegetable Broth,*
  page 48
1/4 cup balsamic or red wine vinegar

3 tbs. sugar
2 tbs. chopped fresh parsley
1/2 tbs. paprika
1 bay leaf
1 tsp. salt
3/4 tsp. dried dill weed
1/2 tsp. dried thyme
1/4 tsp. pepper
1 cup sour cream
chopped fresh parsley for garnish

In a skillet, heat oil and butter on medium-high heat and sauté onions for about 5 minutes, until wilted. Add garlic and sauté for 1 minute. Transfer to the slow cooker along with all remaining ingredients, except sour cream. Cook on high heat for 1 hour. Reduce to low and cook for 6 to 8 hours or until beets are tender. Just before serving, stir in sour cream or serve in dollops on top of the soup. Sprinkle a little chopped parsley for additional garnish.

NAVY BEAN SOUP

Even though this recipe is fat-free, the navy beans naturally impart a rich buttery flavor. Rinsing the beans and replacing the water after the first couple of hours of cooking helps to reduce the gaseous effect. This colorful soup definitely improves with age.

1 lb. dried small white navy beans
12 cups cold water, divided
2 tsp. minced garlic
1 1/2–2 cups chopped onion
2 bay leaves
1 1/2 tbs. salt
1 1/2 tsp. dried oregano

1 tbs. dried basil, or 3 tbs. minced fresh basil
1 can (14 1/2 oz.) chopped tomatoes with juice
1 green bell pepper, cut into 1/2-inch chunks
1/4 cup chopped fresh parsley

Rinse beans in cold water and place in the slow cooker with 7 cups of the water. Cook for 1 hour on high heat. Reduce heat to low and cook for 1 hour. Pour beans into a colander and rinse well. Return to slow cooker and add remaining water, garlic, onion and bay leaves. Set slow cooker on low heat and cook for 2 to 4 hours. Add remaining ingredients and cook for 2 to 4 hours. Taste and adjust seasonings.

BLACK BEAN SOUP

Serve this wonderful soup with a rice side dish and tossed salad. If you wish to reduce the cooking time, soak beans overnight, rinse (to make them less gaseous) and cook beans for 5 to 6 hours on high heat.

1³/₄ cups dried black beans
8 cups water
2 cans (14 ¹/₂ oz.) vegetable broth, or
    4 cups *Vegetable Broth*, page 48
1 tbs. olive oil
1¹/₂ cups diced onions
1 cup diced carrots

³/₄ cup diced red bell peppers
¹/₂ cup diced green onions
1 tbs. minced garlic
2 tsp. ground sage
2 bay leaves
1 tsp. salt
black pepper to taste

Place beans, water and vegetable broth in the slow cooker on low heat. In a skillet, heat olive oil on medium-high heat and cook onions, carrots, red peppers and green onions for about 5 minutes, until wilted.

Transfer vegetables to slow cooker. Add garlic, sage, bay leaves, salt and pepper. Cook on low heat for 10 hours. Taste and determine if beans are tender enough and if you need to add more seasoning. Cook for an additional 2 hours if beans need to be more tender.

SQUASH AND PARSNIP SOUP

This wonderful fall or winter soup is naturally sweet. Serve with a tossed salad, hearty bread and a cobbler or other fruit dessert.

2 lb. butternut squash
1 lb. parsnips, peeled
1 cup water
3 tbs. butter
1 medium onion, thinly sliced

¾ tsp. dried thyme, or more to taste
4 cups *Vegetable Broth,* page 48, or
    canned vegetable broth
salt and pepper to taste
1 cup half-and-half

Cut squash in half and remove seeds. Place a trivet or rack in the bottom of the slow cooker and arrange squash halves cut-side down on trivet. Cut parsnips into 2-inch-square pieces and place in slow cooker. Add water. Cover and cook on high heat for 2 to 3 hours, until vegetables are tender. Melt butter in a medium skillet. Sauté onion until very tender and caramel colored. Remove squash from cooker, remove flesh from shell and discard shell. Cut flesh into small cubes. Puree squash and parsnip in a blender container or food processor workbowl. Add a little water or vegetable broth if needed to help make a smooth puree. Add sautéed onions, thyme, vegetable broth, salt and pepper. Puree until smooth and return to slow cooker. Cook on high heat for 30 minutes or on low heat for 1 to 2 hours. Stir in half-and-half about 15 minutes before serving. Taste and adjust seasonings.

VEGETABLE BROTH

Many of the recipes in this book use vegetable broth. You can buy canned broth or make your own using this recipe. It is important that you strain the vegetables soon after cooking, or the broth will take on a bitter flavor.

2 tbs. butter
6 carrots, quartered
5 stalks celery, quartered
4 medium onions, quartered
1 tsp. tomato paste
2½ qt. cold water
1 tsp. salt
4 peppercorns

In a large skillet, heat butter on medium-high heat and cook carrots, celery and onions until brown. Transfer to the slow cooker. Add tomato paste, water, salt and peppercorns. Cover and cook on low heat for 7 to 9 hours. Taste and cook longer for additional flavor, if desired. Adjust seasonings if desired. Strain mixture through a colander, discard vegetables and refrigerate until ready to use.

CARROT AND ORANGE CHILLED SOUP

This is a good choice for a hot summer day. Garnish with orange slices, grated carrot and chopped fresh mint. Add more ginger if you like a spicier soup.

2 tbs. butter
1/2 tsp. minced fresh ginger, or more to taste
6 carrots, thinly sliced
1/2 cup sliced leeks, white part only, washed
3 cups vegetable broth, divided
1 1/2 cups orange juice
salt and white pepper to taste
orange slices, grated carrot and chopped mint for garnish

In a large saucepan, melt butter on medium-high heat and sauté ginger, carrots and leeks for about 5 minutes, until leeks are soft. Place sautéed vegetables in the slow cooker with 2 cups of the vegetable broth. Cover and cook on high heat for 2 to 3 hours or until carrots are tender.

Transfer to a blender container and puree until smooth. Return pureed mixture to slow cooker and stir in orange juice, salt and white pepper. Add remaining vegetable broth if you prefer a thinner soup. Taste and adjust seasonings. Serve chilled.

FRENCH ONION SOUP

This is a delicious, substantial soup that "wows" them every time. I like to make extra cheese bread to serve alongside.

3 tbs. olive oil
3 tbs. butter
2 lb. onions, sliced
4 medium tomatoes, peeled, seeded and diced
1/4 cup flour
1 tsp. dry mustard
1 tsp. salt
1/8 tsp. white pepper
1/2 cup Sauternes wine
5 cups *Vegetable Broth,* page 48
1 loaf French bread
1 cup shredded Gruyère cheese
1/2–3/4 cup shredded Parmesan cheese
2 large eggs, optional
1/4 cup port wine

Heat olive oil and butter in a skillet on medium heat. Add onions and sauté for about 15 minutes, until onions begin to caramelize and turn brown. Add tomatoes, flour, mustard, salt and white pepper and cook for 1 minute. Add Sauternes and stir until mixture thickens.

Pour mixture into the slow cooker. Add vegetable broth, cover and cook on low heat for 4 to 6 hours.

Cut bread into $\frac{1}{2}$-inch slices. Mix Gruyère and Parmesan cheese together and sprinkle on bread. Broil cheese bread until cheese browns slightly.

Just before serving, beat eggs and mix with Port. Stir mixture into onion soup. Pour soup into bowls and top with toasted cheese bread.

CREAM OF ASPARAGUS SOUP

Servings: 8

Garnish this soup with a small dollop of cream or sour cream in the center with a few steamed asparagus tips floating on top. Hot bread and a crisp carrot salad would be good accompaniments.

1/2 cup butter
2 medium onions, diced
2 lb. potatoes, peeled and diced
3 lb. asparagus, cut into 1-inch pieces,
    tips reserved for garnish

1 qt. *Vegetable Broth,* page 48
2 cups half-and-half
salt and white pepper to taste
1/3 tsp. nutmeg or to taste
cream or sour cream for garnish

In a saucepan, heat butter on medium-high heat and sauté onions for about 5 minutes, until soft. Transfer onions to the slow cooker. Add potatoes, asparagus and vegetable broth. If broth does not cover vegetables, add water to just cover vegetables. Cover and cook on low heat for 6 to 8 hours or until asparagus is tender.

Transfer contents to a blender container and puree until smooth. Return mixture to slow cooker and stir in half-and-half. Add salt, white pepper and nutmeg to taste. Set cooker on high heat and cook for about 15 minutes, until soup is warm enough to serve.

POTATO PEEL BROTH

I use this broth in place of vegetable broth, especially for creamed soups.

7 large baking potatoes
1 large onion, quartered
2 medium carrots, peeled and sliced
1 stalk celery, cut into 1/2-inch pieces
2 whole cloves garlic
1 1/2 qt. cold water

1 large sprig fresh thyme
1 bay leaf
1 small handful fresh parsley stems
cheesecloth and kitchen twine
salt and pepper to taste

Scrub potatoes well and remove peels in 1/2-inch-thick pieces (save potato centers for another use). Place potato peelings, onions, carrots, celery, garlic and water in the slow cooker. Stir to combine.

Place thyme, bay leaf and parsley stems in a 4-inch square piece of cheesecloth and tie with kitchen twine. Add to slow cooker, making sure herb package is submerged in liquid. Cover and cook on low heat for 8 to 9 hours, or on high heat for 4 hours.

Add salt and pepper, taste and adjust seasonings. Immediately strain mixture through a colander, cover and store broth in the refrigerator until ready to use. Discard strained vegetables.

PROVENÇAL VEGETABLE SOUP

Servings: 8–10

This is a special French vegetable soup with an added touch of pistou. Pistou is a garlic paste made from mashed garlic, Parmesan cheese, olive oil, basil and tomato paste. Serve this soup with hot, crusty French bread. For variety, add ½ cup orzo or broken pasta when adding the zucchini.

1 large leek, cleaned and thinly sliced
1 medium onion, diced
2 cups 1-inch green bean pieces
2 cups diced potatoes
2 cups diced peeled carrots
2 cups diced tomatoes
2½ qt. cold water
1 tbs. salt
freshly ground pepper to taste
2 small zucchini, diced

¼–½ lb. mushrooms, sliced
1 tbs. minced garlic
2 tbs. chopped fresh basil, or 2 tsp. dried
salt for sprinkling
1 can (6 oz.) tomato paste
¼ cup grated Parmesan cheese
¼ cup olive oil
shredded Parmesan cheese for garnish

Place leek, onion, green beans, potatoes, carrots, tomatoes, water, salt and pepper in the slow cooker. Cover and cook on low heat for 8 to 9 hours, or on high heat for 4 hours, until vegetables are crisp-tender. Add zucchini and mushroom and cook on high heat for 30 minutes or until mushrooms are tender.

While soup is cooking, make pistou: Mash garlic, basil and a sprinkling of salt with a mortar and pestle, or press with a knife. Work in tomato paste, Parmesan cheese and olive oil to form a smooth paste. Add a small amount of soup to mashed garlic mixture and mix until smooth. Stir into soup. Taste and adjust seasonings. Serve with a sprinkling of Parmesan cheese for garnish.

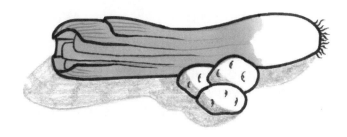

LENTIL SOUP WITH SWISS CHEESE

Servings: 4–6

This soup is best left to sit overnight to allow the flavors to meld. Serve with a good rye bread, a vegetable salad, and a light dessert like a lemon mousse or dessert soufflé.

1 tsp. olive oil
1/3 cup dry white wine
1 1/2 cups chopped onions
1 cup chopped carrots
2 cups seeded, chopped tomatoes
1/2 tsp. dried thyme
1/2 tsp. dried marjoram
1 cup dried lentils

3 cups *Vegetable Broth,* page 48
3 tbs. miso paste, dissolved in 1/2 cup water
pepper to taste, optional
1 cup grated Swiss cheese
1/4 cup chopped green onions
1/4 cup grated carrots

In a saucepan, heat olive oil on medium-high heat. Add wine and onions and cook for 5 minutes, until onions are soft.

Transfer onions to the slow cooker. Add carrots, tomatoes, thyme, marjoram, lentils and vegetable broth. Cover and cook on low heat for 9 to 10 hours. Add miso paste and pepper before serving. Miso has a salty taste, so add sparingly to taste. Sprinkle a little cheese in serving bowls, ladle in soup and garnish with green onions and carrots.

SPINACH POTATO SOUP

This is a healthy, hearty soup ideal for the cold season. Serve with multi-grain bread, cooked carrots and a warm fruited dessert like cobbler or pie.

1/4 cup olive oil
3 large leeks, white part only, washed
1 lb. russet potatoes, peeled and diced
1 tbs. minced garlic, or to taste
6 cups *Vegetable Broth*, page 48
1 tbs. salt

2 tsp. lemon juice
3/4 tsp. white pepper
1 pinch nutmeg
3/4 lb. fresh spinach, stems removed
1/3 cup crème fraiche or sour cream
chopped green onions for garnish

Heat olive oil in a skillet on medium heat and sauté leeks for about 4 to 5 minutes, until soft. Transfer to the slow cooker. Add potatoes, garlic, vegetable broth, salt, lemon juice, white pepper and nutmeg. Cover and cook on low heat for 8 to 9 hours, until potatoes are tender. Add fresh spinach to soup. Stir a little of the hot soup in with crème fraiche to prevent curdling and then add crème fraiche to soup. Cook for 10 minutes and serve. Garnish soup with a sprinkling of chopped green onions.

Note: If fresh spinach is not available, use 1 package (10 oz.) frozen spinach, thawed and squeezed dry.

ROASTED RED PEPPER SOUP

This tasty and colorful soup combines eggplant, red peppers and leeks. Serve with crisp crackers or crusty bread and fruit salad. Large shavings of a hard cheese like Parmesan or Romano give this soup great eye appeal.

4 red bell peppers
2½ lb. eggplant
3–4 tbs. olive oil
1½ cups chopped onions
2 cups chopped leeks, mostly white parts
1 tbs. minced garlic
8–9 cups vegetable broth
3 tbs. tomato paste
¼ cup chopped fresh basil, or 4 tsp. dried
2 tsp. dried thyme
salt and pepper to taste
¼ cup butter
1¾ tsp. lemon juice
fresh Parmesan or Romano cheese shavings for garnish

Cut peppers in half, remove seeds, and roast under a broiler until skins are blackened. Place blackened peppers in a paper bag for 10 minutes. Remove skins and cut into a coarse dice.

Peel eggplants, cut into ¾-inch slices and place slices on a baking sheet. Place under a broiler and brown on both sides. Cut into ¾-inch squares.

Heat olive oil in a skillet on medium-high heat and sauté onions, leeks and garlic for about 3 to 4 minutes, until soft.

Transfer onion mixture, roasted red peppers and eggplant cubes to the slow cooker. Add vegetable broth, tomato paste, basil, thyme, salt and pepper. Cover and cook on low heat for 6 to 8 hours.

Remove soup from slow cooker and puree in a blender until smooth. You will need to do this in batches. Return soup to slow cooker. Set cooker on high heat and stir in butter until melted. Add lemon juice, taste and adjust seasonings. Serve soup with large shavings of Parmesan or Romano cheese.

CHIPOTLE CORN SOUP

Chipotle chiles are usually canned in a tomato sauce and found in the Mexican or specialty food sections of supermarkets. Be aware that a little goes a long way. Start by adding the minimum amount and add more, if desired, just before serving.

2 tbs. butter
3/4 cup chopped onions
1 large red bell pepper, seeded and diced
1 1/2 tsp. minced garlic
1 can (14 1/2 oz.) diced tomatoes with juice
2 cans (14 3/4 oz. each) cream-style corn
2 cups water
1/2–1 1/2 tbs. chopped canned chipotle chiles
1 pkg. (16 oz.) frozen or fresh corn
1 cup cream
1–2 tbs. chopped fresh cilantro
1 tsp. dried oregano
salt and pepper to taste, optional
chopped fresh cilantro for garnish, optional

In a skillet on medium-high heat, melt butter and sauté onions and bell peppers for about 5 minutes, until soft. Add garlic and cook for 1 minute.

Transfer vegetables to the slow cooker. Add tomatoes and creamed corn.

In a blender, puree water and ½ tbs. of the chipotle chiles until well mixed. Stir chipotle mixture into slow cooker. Cover and cook on low heat for 3 to 4 hours, or on high heat for 1 to 2 hours.

About 15 to 30 minutes before serving, stir in corn, cream, cilantro and oregano. Taste and add salt, pepper and additional seasonings if desired. If you like it really hot, add more chipotle chiles.

ANGOSTURA BEAN SOUP

Angostura bitters has a slight clove scent. Angostura bitters is generally used in making cocktails, but can be added to sauces with a strong flavor, such as mustard sauce.

2½ cups dried small white beans
water to cover beans
1 qt. water
1 tbs. butter
1 cup diced onions

1 tsp. salt
⅛ tsp. black pepper
1 bay leaf
1 tbs. angostura bitters
½ cup ketchup

Place beans in a bowl, cover with water and soak overnight. Cover and cook on high heat for 1½ to 2 hours.

In a colander, drain beans, rinse and add to the slow cooker with 1 quart water. Heat butter in a skillet on medium-high heat and sauté onions until translucent.

Add sautéed onions to slow cooker with salt, pepper and bay leaf. Cook on low heat for 4 to 6 hours or until beans are tender. Add angostura bitters and ketchup about 30 minutes before serving. Remove bay leaf before serving. Taste and adjust seasonings.

ONION BISQUE

A good accompaniment for this dish would be Confetti Rice and Vegetables, *page 16, some hearty bread and a tossed green salad. Minced chives make a good garnish.*

4 medium leeks
2 tbs. olive oil
3 tbs. butter
5 shallots, minced
4 medium onions, coarsely diced
4 tsp. minced garlic
4 baking potatoes, peeled and cut into
  1/2-inch cubes

2 tsp. salt
1 tsp. dried basil
1 tsp. dried oregano
1/2 tsp. dried marjoram
2 bay leaves
6 cups *Vegetable Broth*, page 48
pepper to taste, optional

Cut tough top leaves from leeks about 2 inches above slit. Cut leeks in half lengthwise and thoroughly wash out dirt between leaves. Cut into 1/4-inch pieces. In a large skillet on medium-high heat, heat oil and butter and sauté leeks, shallots and onions for 5 to 6 minutes, until soft. Add garlic and sauté for 1 minute. Pour into the slow cooker. Add potatoes, salt, basil, oregano, marjoram, bay leaves and vegetable broth. Cover and cook on low heat for 8 hours. Taste, adjust seasonings and add pepper if desired.

SIDE DISHES

POTATOES IN SPAGHETTI SAUCE

There are a large variety of bottled sauces on the market today. I prefer meatless basil and tomato sauce and usually throw in a handful of chopped fresh basil. Of course, you can always use your favorite spaghetti sauce recipe.

8–10 large baking potatoes
1 jar (26 oz.) meatless spaghetti sauce
1 tsp. minced garlic
3/4 cup chopped onion
2 tbs. chopped fresh parsley
2 tbs. chopped fresh basil or oregano, optional
1 cup grated Parmesan cheese for sprinkling, optional

Peel potatoes and cut into 1 1/2-inch chunks. Place potatoes, spaghetti sauce, garlic, onions, parsley and basil or oregano in the slow cooker. Cook on low heat for 10 hours, or on high heat for 4 hours, until potatoes are tender. Sprinkle top of sauced potatoes with Parmesan cheese.

CAPONATA

This is an Italian vegetable combination that gets its special flavor from grilling the vegetables before cooking. Use this recipe as a side dish or on toasted or fresh bread as an appetizer.

1 medium eggplant
1 tsp. salt
1 green bell pepper
2 small zucchini
3 tbs. olive oil, divided
1 tbs. butter
1 cup diced sweet or red onion
1 tsp. minced garlic
2 cups chopped fresh or canned
    tomatoes
1/2 cup chopped celery

3 tbs. balsamic or red wine vinegar
1 tbs. sugar
1 tbs. tomato paste
1/3 cup chopped green olives or Greek
    olives
1 tbs. capers
3 tbs. fresh basil, or 1 tbs. dried
1 tbs. fresh oregano, or 1 tsp. dried
3/4 tsp. black pepper
salt to taste

Slice eggplant into $1/2$-inch rounds, place on a towel, sprinkle with salt and set aside for 30 minutes. Cut green pepper in half and remove seeds. Cut zucchini into 1-inch slices. Rinse salt from eggplant rounds and pat dry. Brush both sides of eggplant, green pepper and zucchini with 2 tbs. of the olive oil and place on a grill or under the broiler until vegetables are browned on both sides. Cut all grilled vegetables into 1-inch chunks and set aside.

In a skillet, heat remaining 1 tbs. oil and butter on medium-high heat. Sauté onions for about 5 minutes, until wilted. Stir in garlic and sauté for 1 minute.

Transfer to the slow cooker. Add tomatoes, celery, vinegar, sugar, tomato paste, olives, capers, basil, oregano, pepper and salt. Cook on low heat for 4 to 5 hours. Add grilled vegetables and cook for 1 to 2 hours, until vegetables are tender. Taste and adjust seasonings. Serve this dish either hot or at room temperature.

EASY SCALLOPED POTATOES

Servings: 4–6

This easy recipe can be put together quickly. The taste can vary with the flavor of soup you use. If you use cream of mushroom, add ½ tsp. Worcestershire sauce to enhance the flavor of the mushrooms. If you wish to make a more substantial dish, sauté 1 cup sliced mushrooms in a little butter and layer the mushrooms with the potatoes.

1 can (10½ oz.) condensed cheddar cheese, cream of celery or cream of mushroom soup
¾ cup milk or evaporated milk
pepper to taste

4 cups peeled, thinly sliced baking potatoes
1 small onion, thinly sliced
2 tbs. butter
1 dash paprika

In a bowl, combine condensed soup, milk and pepper.

Line the slow cooker with foil (enough to fold over the top). Place ½ of the potatoes in cooker and sprinkle with ½ of the onions and ½ of the soup mixture. Repeat with remaining potatoes, onion and soup mixture. Dot with butter and sprinkle with paprika.

Overlap top with foil, cover and cook on low heat for 10 to 12 hours, or on high heat for 3 to 4 hours. Potatoes should be fork-tender when done.

RED CABBAGE WITH FRUIT AND ONIONS

Servings: 4–6

Cabbage marries well with fruit. This recipe would go well with stuffed baked potatoes, a green vegetable and a chocolate dessert. If fresh raspberries are not available, use frozen. You may have to increase the sugar.

1/2 cup butter
1/2 cup chopped shallots
2 cups finely sliced onion
 (prefer sweet variety)
2 cups peeled, thinly sliced tart apples
 (prefer Pippin or Granny Smith)

1 medium red cabbage, thinly sliced
3/4 cup raspberry vinegar
1/2 cup sugar, or more to taste
salt and pepper to taste
2 cups fresh raspberries

In a large skillet, melt butter and sauté shallots and onions for 5 minutes on medium, until onions are soft and beginning to brown.

Transfer onion mixture to the slow cooker. Add apple, cabbage, vinegar, sugar, salt and pepper. Cover and cook on low heat for 6 to 7 hours. Add raspberries and cook for another 30 minutes. Taste and adjust seasonings and sweetness.

SWEET POTATOES AND APPLES

This very simple recipe is sweetened with honey. Serve with a crunchy green vegetable, carrot and cabbage slaw and a lemon dessert.

2½ lb. sweet potatoes or yams
1 lb. tart apples (prefer Granny Smith
   or Pippin)
1 tbs. fresh lemon juice
¼ cup butter, melted
½ cup honey

½ tsp. salt
½ tsp. cinnamon
¼ tsp. ground ginger
¼ tsp. nutmeg
1 pinch ground cloves

Peel sweet potatoes and cut into ¼-inch slices. Core and cut apples into ¼-inch slices. Toss apples in a bowl with lemon juice to prevent discoloring. Place sweet potatoes and apples in the slow cooker.

In a bowl, combine butter, honey, salt, cinnamon, ginger, nutmeg and cloves. Pour butter mixture into slow cooker and stir to coat potatoes and apples. Cover and cook on low heat for 8 to 10 hours, or on high heat for 4 hours, until potatoes are tender.

CUMIN RICE WITH NUTS

This very simple recipe goes well with bean dishes and vegetable casseroles. Toasting the nuts enhances their flavor and helps prevent them from becoming soggy. If desired, add $1/2$ cup dried currants or raisins.

6 tbs. butter, divided
2 cups long-grain rice
$1^3/_4$ tsp. salt
4 tsp. ground cumin
4 cups water
$3/_4$ cup pine nuts or chopped almonds

In a skillet on medium-high heat, melt 4 tbs. of the butter and add rice, stirring until rice turns light brown. Transfer rice to the slow cooker with salt, cumin and water. Cover and cook on high heat for 2 to 3 hours, or on low heat for 9 hours.

Melt remaining 2 tbs. butter in skillet on medium-high heat, add pine nuts and stir until browned. Stir into rice mixture and serve immediately.

CHEESY GRITS

Servings: 6-8

Grits are generally bland and need the "zing" of cheese. I like to mix the flavor of cheeses for variety. If you like a little more color, add a 2 oz. jar of drained red pimientos.

4 cups water
1 cup corn grits
½ cup butter
1 tsp. seasoning salt
2 large eggs
4 oz. grated cheddar cheese

4 oz. grated Muenster, Gruyère or
   Monterey Jack cheese
1 tbs. chopped fresh parsley
salt to taste, optional
grated Parmesan cheese for garnish

In a saucepan on high heat, bring water to boil and stir in grits. Cook for 5 minutes, stirring constantly. Stir in butter until melted.

Transfer to the slow cooker. Stir in seasoning salt, eggs, and cheeses (If using an egg substitute, add during the last 10 minutes of cooking). Cook on low heat for 3 to 4 hours, stirring occasionally. Before serving, stir in parsley and salt if desired. Sprinkle with Parmesan cheese for garnish.

MUSHROOM AND TOMATO RICE

This is a tasty rice pilaf that would go well with bean dishes and a nut loaf. To vary the dish, use different varieties of mushrooms, or add minced garlic or ½ tsp. of basil, thyme or herb of choice.

¼ cup butter, divided
¾ lb. mushrooms, sliced and stems
   separated from caps
1 medium onion, finely chopped
1¼ cups long-grain rice
2½ cups *Vegetable Broth,* page 48

½ tsp. salt
freshly ground pepper to taste
1 tbs. fresh lemon juice
1 large tomato, peeled, seeded and
   chopped
2 tbs. finely chopped fresh parsley

Melt 2 tbs. of the butter on medium-high heat in a skillet and sauté mushroom stems with onions until vegetables are wilted. Add rice and stir until rice becomes translucent.

Transfer to the slow cooker. Add vegetable broth, salt and pepper. Cook on high heat for 2 to 3 hours.

In a skillet on medium-high heat, heat remaining 2 tbs. butter and sauté sliced mushroom caps until soft. Gently stir mushroom caps and tomatoes into cooked rice. Taste and adjust seasonings.

ULTIMATE WILD RICE

Wild rice has a wonderful earthy flavor and chewy texture. Caramelized walnuts and essence of orange transform this side dish into a delicious treat.

2 cups wild rice
2 qt. *Vegetable Broth,* page 48
$^1/_2$ cup butter, divided
$^1/_4$ cup finely chopped shallots
3 stalks celery, finely chopped

3 tbs. grated orange zest
1 cup chopped walnuts
$^1/_4$ cup sugar
salt and pepper to taste, optional

Wash rice, drain and place in the slow cooker with broth. In a saucepan on medium-high heat, melt $^1/_4$ cup of the butter and sauté shallots and celery until soft.

Transfer shallots and celery to slow cooker. Add orange zest. Cover and cook on high heat for 2 to 3 hours, or on low heat for 6 to 7 hours.

Caramelize nuts by melting remaining $^1/_4$ cup butter in a skillet on medium-high heat. Stir in walnuts and reduce heat to medium. Sprinkle sugar over walnuts and stir until sugar has caramelized. Remove from heat as soon as nuts brown. Gently stir nuts into rice and serve immediately.

ROSEMARY CREAMED ONIONS

Servings: 6

Take advantage of the season and use sweet onions like Walla Walla or Vidalia of they are available. Serve these onions as an accompaniment to a nut loaf, Bulgur Pilaf with Garbanzo Beans, *page 21, or* White Bean Stew, *page 20, along with a colorful salad or steamed crisp-tender vegetables.*

6 large yellow or sweet variety onions
2 cups vegetable broth
2–3 tbs. extra virgin olive oil
salt and pepper to taste
2 tbs. chopped fresh rosemary, or 2 tsp. dried
1 cup heavy cream

Cut onions in half and place cut-side up in the slow cooker. Pour vegetable broth into cooker. Brush onions with olive oil and liberally sprinkle with salt and pepper. Add rosemary, cover and cook on low heat for 8 to 10 hours, until onions are tender. Pour in cream and cook for 1 hour on low heat or until cream thickens. Taste and adjust seasonings.

GLAZED PINEAPPLE CARROTS

Servings: 6

This is a yummy, quick recipe that even kids can appreciate! This would go well with Eggplant Parmesan Casserole, *page 12,* Confetti Rice and Vegetables, *page 16, or* Bulgur Pilaf with Garbanzo Beans, *page 21.*

6 large carrots, peeled and thinly sliced
1 cup crushed pineapple, drained
1/4 cup butter
1/2 cup orange juice
1/2 cup brown sugar, packed
pepper to taste, optional

Place carrots, pineapple, butter, orange juice, and brown sugar in the slow cooker. Cover and cook on high for 2 to 3 hours, until carrots are tender. Taste and add pepper if desired.

TURNIP AND ONION CASSEROLE

Servings: 6

Double-cooking the turnips brings out their natural sweetness. Serve this dish with a colorful tossed salad or mixed steamed vegetables.

2 1/2 lb. turnips
1 1/2 cups *Vegetable Broth,* page 48
1 tbs. chopped onion
2 tbs. chopped fresh parsley
3/4 cup applesauce

1/8 tsp. pepper, or to taste
1/4 cup butter, melted, divided
1 cup dried breadcrumbs or crushed
   croutons
salt to taste

Peel turnips, dice and place in the slow cooker with vegetable broth and onion. Cover and cook on low heat for 6 to 8 hours, or on high heat for 2 to 3 hours, until turnips are very tender.

Mash turnip mixture until smooth. Add parsley, applesauce, pepper and 1/2 of the melted butter. Taste and add salt if desired. Return mixture to slow cooker.

In a bowl, combine remaining butter and breadcrumbs. Sprinkle turnip mixture with buttered crumbs. Cover and cook on low heat for 1 to 2 hours.

BROWN SUGAR-GLAZED ONIONS

Servings: 6-8

This great side dish would go well with Mixed Nut Loaf, *page 8, lentils, or* Cashew and Rice Loaf, *page 22. Carrots can be substituted for the onions: just skip the step of boiling the vegetable before adding to the slow cooker.*

2 lb. small white onions
boiling salted water to cover
1/2 cup butter, melted
1/2 cup brown sugar, packed
2 tbs. fresh lemon juice

1 tsp. salt, or to taste
1/2 tsp. ground ginger
white pepper to taste
1 cup water

In a large saucepan, cook onions in boiling salted water for 15 minutes.

Place butter, sugar, lemon juice, salt, ginger, white pepper and water in the slow cooker and whisk until well mixed.

Drain onions and transfer to slow cooker. Stir to coat onions, cover and cook on low heat for 6 to 8 hours, or on high heat for 2 to 3 hours. Remove lid and allow water to evaporate for 20 to 30 minutes before serving.

YAM AND APPLE CRUNCH

This is a fast recipe using canned yams and the natural sweetness of apple. The crunch mixture is added just before serving. Cooked sweet potatoes can be substituted for the yams.

6 cups sliced tart apples
1 can (1 lb.) yams
1 1/2 tbs. grated orange zest
1/2 cup brown sugar, packed
1/2 tsp. cinnamon

1/2 tsp. salt
1 pinch nutmeg
6 tbs. butter, melted, divided
1 1/2 cups unsweetened cereal flakes

Peel, core and thickly slice apples. Place apples, yams and orange zest in the slow cooker and stir to combine.

In a small bowl, combine brown sugar, cinnamon, salt and nutmeg. Pour 1/2 of the sugar mixture over yam mixture. Drizzle 3 tbs. of the butter over yams, cover and cook on low heat for 6 hours.

Mix cereal flakes, remaining butter and remaining sugar mixture together. Transfer yam and apple mixture to a serving bowl, sprinkle with cereal mixture and serve.

ROQUEFORT POTATOES

Servings: 6

Roquefort cheese adds a pleasant tang to stuffed potatoes. This would be good served with Mixed Nut Loaf, *page 8,* Many Bean Chili, *page 14, or* Picadillo Sweet Beans, *page 18. Blue cheese can be substituted for Roquefort, if desired.*

6 baking potatoes, unpeeled
1 cup sour cream
$1/4$ cup butter, melted
$1/4$ cup milk, or more to taste
3 oz. crumbled Roquefort cheese
2 tbs. minced fresh chives
1 tsp. salt, or more to taste
pepper to taste
$1/4$ cup crumbled soy bacon, optional

Wash potatoes but do not dry, place in the slow cooker, cover and cook on low heat for 6 to 8 hours. When potatoes are fork-tender, remove from slow cooker and cut in half.

Cut a small opening at the top of each potato, scoop out center of potato and save the shell. Place potato centers in a mixer bowl with sour cream, melted butter and milk and beat until smooth. If you prefer a thinner filling, add more milk. Add Roquefort cheese, chives, salt and pepper and mix lightly. Taste and adjust seasonings.

Spoon filling into shells. Shape the top of each into a mound.

Place potatoes on a baking pan and bake in a 425° oven for 15 minutes before serving. If desired, sprinkle top with crumbled soy bacon before serving.

Note: If an oven is not available, place stuffed potatoes in slow cooker, cover and cook on high heat for 45 to 60 minutes.

NUT-STUFFED ONIONS

Sweet onions are a must when making stuffed onions. I prefer Walla Walla Sweets or Vidalias. Almonds or cashews can be substituted for the hazelnuts.

6 large sweet onions
1 tbs. olive oil
2 tbs. butter
3/4 cup chopped mushrooms
1/2 cup finely chopped carrots
1/3 tsp. pepper
1/2 cup apple juice
3/4 cup chopped apple (tart variety preferred)
1/2 cup cooked long-grain rice
1/2 cup chopped toasted hazelnuts
1/4 tsp. salt, or to taste
1 cup soft breadcrumbs
1 tbs. chopped fresh basil, or 1 tsp. dried
1/2 cup water
1 tbs. butter, melted

Leave skins on onions. Cut a thin slice from bottom of each onion to make a flat surface. Scoop out centers, leaving a $1/3$-inch-thick shell. Reserve enough onion centers to make $1/3$ cup chopped onion for filling.

Brush outside of onions with oil. In a skillet, melt butter on medium heat. Add reserved $1/3$ cup chopped onion, mushrooms, carrots and pepper and stir for 5 minutes. Add apple juice, apple, rice, nuts and salt and cook for 1 minute. Remove skillet from heat and stir in $1/2$ of the breadcrumbs and basil. Spoon filling into onion shells.

Wrap each onion tightly in foil. Place onions on a trivet or rack in the bottom of the slow cooker and add $1/2$ cup water. Cook on high for 4 to 5 hours, until fork-tender.

Remove onions from cooker, unwrap and set upright in a boiler-proof baking dish. Mix remaining breadcrumbs with melted butter and sprinkle on top of onions.

Place onions under a broiler until breadcrumbs are slightly browned. If desired, remove peelings before serving.

CREAMY BARLEY

Barley acts like Arborio rice: the starch forms a creamy sauce. For a change, try adding sautéed mushrooms, several colors of sautéed bell peppers or artichokes.

2 tbs. olive oil
1/2 cup chopped onions
1 tsp. minced garlic
1 cup pearl barley
3/4 cup dry white wine
6 cups *Vegetable Broth*, page 48
3 tbs. butter

2 tbs. lemon juice
3 tbs. chopped fresh parsley
2 tsp. chopped fresh chives
1 tsp. dried chervil
salt and pepper to taste
1/2–3/4 cup freshly grated Parmesan
    cheese

In a skillet on medium-high heat, heat olive oil and sauté onions until soft. Add garlic and barley and cook for 1 minute. Pour in wine and cook until most of wine is absorbed. Transfer mixture to the slow cooker.

Add 4 cups of the broth, stir to combine, cover and cook on low heat for 4 hours. Stir and determine if you wish to add up to 2 more cups vegetable broth to make barley more creamy.

Add butter, lemon juice, parsley, chives, chervil, salt and pepper. Cook for 2 to 4 hours. Just before serving, stir in Parmesan cheese. Taste and adjust seasonings.

BRAISED ARTICHOKES

Baby artichokes are so tender that the centers can be eaten. If the baby variety is not available, use 4 large artichokes, which should be trimmed, cut into quarters and the center chokes removed.

24 baby artichokes
2 tbs. lemon juice
water to cover
$1/4$ cup extra virgin olive oil
6 sprigs fresh thyme, or $1/2$ tsp. dried

1 tsp. grated lemon zest
salt and black pepper to taste
2 large whole cloves garlic
2 bay leaves
2 tbs. chopped fresh cilantro or parsley

Trim artichokes by removing any tough outer leaves. Trim base and slice off top third of each artichoke. If there are any sharp points on leaves, cut them off with a scissors. Place artichokes in a bowl, sprinkle with lemon juice and cover with water to help prevent discoloration. Place $1/2$ of the olive oil, thyme leaves and lemon zest in the slow cooker with artichokes and $2^1/2$ cups of the lemon water. Add garlic, bay leaves, salt and pepper. Cover and cook on high heat for 3 to 5 hours or until artichokes are tender. Remove artichokes to a serving dish and transfer liquid from slow cooker to a saucepan. On high heat, reduce liquid to $1/2$ cup. Pour reduced liquid over artichokes, sprinkle with remaining olive oil, pepper and more salt if desired. Sprinkle with cilantro or parsley and serve.

CEREALS AND BREAKFAST BREADS

DATE CORNMEAL MUSH

This cereal is filling and delicious. In place of dates, you can use raisins or dried fruit of your choice. Kids like to stir in a little peanut butter for a pleasant change.

2 cups cornmeal
6 cups water
1 tsp. salt
$\frac{1}{2}$ cup chopped dates
$\frac{1}{4}$ cup brown sugar, date sugar, honey or fruit concentrate, or more to taste
$\frac{1}{2}$ cup chopped toasted walnuts, optional

Place cornmeal, water, salt, dates and sugar in the slow cooker. Cook for 8 to 9 hours on low heat. Stir in walnuts just before serving.

FRUIT AND NUT BARLEY CEREAL

A wonderful fruity cereal is delicately flavored with coriander. Stir in the almonds just before serving to keep them from becoming soft.

1 cup barley
2 qt. water
1 tsp. salt
2 cups chopped dried mixed fruit
1 cup raisins
$1/2$ tsp. ground coriander
1 cup almonds

Place barley, water, salt, mixed fruit, raisins and coriander in the slow cooker. Set on low heat and cook for 8 to 9 hours.

Toast almonds in a 350° oven for about 10 minutes, until nuts are lightly browned. Chop nuts and stir them into cereal just before serving.

FRUITED MILLET CEREAL

Millet is a healthy grain that is often overlooked. Toasting the millet gives it a delightful, nutty flavor. I like to use a sweet variety of apple like Golden Delicious or Criterion.

1 cup millet
1 qt. water
1 tsp. salt
1 medium apple, peeled and diced
1 cup raisins
$1/2$ cup coconut, sweetened or unsweetened

Place all ingredients in the slow cooker and stir. Cover, set cooker on low heat and cook for 8 to 9 hours.

BROWN RICE AND RAISINS

For a change, try using chopped dates, craisins (sweetened dried cranberries) or chopped mixed dried fruit.

2 cups brown rice
4 cups water
1 cup raisins
$1/2$ tsp. salt
$1/4$ tsp. ground cardamom
$1/4$ tsp. ground coriander

Place all ingredients in the slow cooker, cover and cook on low heat for 8 to 9 hours. Taste and adjust seasonings.

HOT CEREAL WITH SESAME SALT (GOMASHIO)

Servings: 4

Gomashio is ground toasted sesame seeds mixed with salt. The Japanese like to use it on rice, but it tastes wonderful on all cooked grains. If you use cereals other than oats—like muesli or alternative grains—follow package directions on the amount of water needed. The gomashio recipe will make more than is needed for this amount of cereal. Store in a tightly covered container.

1¾ cups steel-cut oats
5 cups water
⅔ cup sesame seeds
4 tsp. salt

Stir oats and water together, cover and cook on low heat for 8 hours.

Roast sesame seeds and salt in a heavy skillet over medium heat for about 3 minutes, until seeds become a light golden brown.

Using a mortar and pestle or a small electric food grinder, coarsely grind sesame seed mixture but do not turn it to a powder; it should have a chewy texture. Sprinkle some on your cereal and keep the rest sealed in a glass jar.

RHUBARB COFFEECAKE

Servings: 8

This is a scrumptious breakfast food that would go well with fresh fruit. When rhubarb is not available, use cranberries or blueberries. Be sure to taste and adjust the sweetness of the filling before adding it to cake batter.

FILLING

4 cups 1-inch rhubarb pieces
3/4 cup sugar, or to taste
1/4 cup flour

3 tbs. butter
2 tsp. cinnamon
1/4 tsp. nutmeg

BATTER

3/4 cup butter
1 cup sugar
2 large eggs
1 1/2 tsp. vanilla extract
1 1/2 cups white flour
1/2 cup whole wheat flour

1 1/2 tsp. baking powder
1/4 tsp. salt
1/4 tsp. baking soda
1 1/2 tbs. grated lemon zest
1 cup plain yogurt

TOPPING

½ cup butter	1 ½ tsp. cinnamon
1 cup brown sugar, packed	1 cup white flour

Butter and flour a 9-inch springform pan or a baking pan that will fit in your slow cooker.

To make filling: In a bowl, combine rhubarb, sugar, flour, butter, cinnamon and nutmeg.

To make batter: With a mixer, beat butter and sugar together until fluffy; beat in eggs and vanilla. In a bowl, mix together flour, whole-wheat flour, baking powder, salt and baking soda. Mix lemon zest with yogurt. Stir ½ of the flour mixture into butter mixture. Add ½ of the yogurt mixture and stir in. Stir in remainder of flour mixture; stir in remainder of yogurt mixture. Do not overbeat.

To make topping: Mix butter, sugar, cinnamon and flour together in a bowl until crumbly and set aside.

Place ½ of the batter in prepared springform pan and cover with filling. Cover with remaining batter and sprinkle with topping. Cover with several layers of paper towels and set baking dish directly into slow cooker. Cover and cook on high heat for 2 to 3 hours. Test by inserting knife in center. Knife should come out clean. Serve hot or at room temperature.

PUMPKIN DATE BREAD

Makes 2 loaves

I like to serve this bread with tea. For a change, use orange juice in place of water and add 1 tbs. grated orange zest. If you like it rich, serve with a flavored cream cheese spread or butter.

4 eggs
2/3 cup butter
1 1/2 cups brown sugar, packed
1 1/3 cups granulated sugar
1 can (16 oz.) pumpkin
2/3 cup water
3 1/2 cups flour
2 tsp. baking soda
1 tsp. salt
1 tsp. cinnamon

1/2 tsp. ground cloves
1/2 tsp. ground ginger
1/2 tsp. baking powder
1/4 tsp. nutmeg
1 pinch ground allspice
1 cup chopped toasted walnuts
1 cup chopped dates, raisins or dried cranberries
2 cups hot water

In a bowl, combine eggs, butter, brown sugar and sugar until well mixed. Stir in pumpkin and water. Add flour, baking soda, salt, cinnamon, cloves, ginger, baking powder, nutmeg and allspice. Stir until well mixed and gently stir in dates and nuts.

Grease two 1-pound coffee cans or a large baking dish and pour in pumpkin mixture. Cover with foil and tie with string.

Place filled cans on a metal rack in the slow cooker and add 2 cups hot water. Cover and cook on high heat for 2½ to 3 hours, or until a knife inserted in the center comes out clean. Allow bread to cool for 10 minutes before removing.

ZUCCHINI NUT BREAD

Makes 2 loaves

This wonderful, moist bread can have many variations. Carrots can be substituted for zucchini, and toasted pecans for walnuts. Add 1 tbs. lemon or orange zest for flavor and/or 1 cup shredded coconut for flavor and texture.

2 cups sugar
1 cup vegetable oil
3 large eggs
2 tsp. vanilla extract
3 cups flour
1 tsp. baking soda
1 tsp. baking powder
$\frac{1}{2}$ tsp. salt
$\frac{1}{2}$ tsp. cinnamon
$\frac{1}{4}$ tsp. nutmeg
2 cups grated unpeeled zucchini
1 cup chopped toasted walnuts
2 cups hot water

In a large bowl, beat together sugar and oil. Add eggs and vanilla and beat until well mixed.

In a separate bowl, mix flour, baking soda, baking powder, salt, cinnamon and nutmeg. Stir into egg mixture. Gently fold in zucchini and nuts. Grease two 1-pound coffee cans (or a large baking dish). Pour bread mixture into cans, cover with foil and tie with string.

Place cans on a trivet or rack in the slow cooker and add 2 cups hot water. Cover and cook on high heat for 2½ to 3 hours or until a knife inserted in the center comes out clean.

SOUR CREAM BANANA BREAD

Makes 1 loaf

This moist bread is ideal for breakfast, brunch or afternoon tea. I like to use banana extract, but vanilla extract can be substituted.

1 cup sugar
½ cup vegetable oil
2 large eggs
1 cup mashed ripe bananas
½ cup sour cream
1 tsp. banana or vanilla extract
1 ½ cups flour

1 tsp. baking soda
1 tsp. baking powder
½ tsp. salt
½ cup chopped walnuts or pecans,
    optional
2 cups hot water

With a mixer, beat sugar and oil together until smooth. Add eggs, bananas, sour cream and banana extract, blending well. In a bowl, mix together flour, baking soda, baking powder and salt. Gently stir into banana mixture. Add nuts if desired.

Butter a 1-pound coffee can and pour batter into can. Cover can with foil and tie with string. Place can on a trivet or rack in the slow cooker and add 2 cups hot water.

Cover and cook on low heat for 2 to 3 hours or until a knife inserted in the center comes out clean.

BEVERAGES, SAUCES AND CHUTNEYS

HOT FRUIT PUNCH

Makes 5½ quarts

This wonderful mixture of fruit juices and spices is ideal for fall and winter months. If you wish to add "spike" to your punch, serve vodka or tequila alongside. Liquor must be added when the punch is served, or the cooking process will reduce the alcohol content of the punch.

3 cans (6 oz.) frozen lemonade, undiluted
6 cups orange juice
6 cups cranberry juice
8 cups apple cider
5 cinnamon sticks, 3 inches each
1 tbs. whole cloves
1¼ tbs. whole allspice
1 orange, sliced
1 lemon, sliced

Place all ingredients in the slow cooker, cover and cook on low heat for 2 to 5 hours. Remove orange and lemon slices if punch becomes too strong.

SPICED GRAPE PUNCH

Grape juice is a popular flavor among adults and kids. A good substitute for red grape juice is nonalcoholic grape juice, made with the same grapes used in wine-making.

1 ½ qt. red grape juice
1 qt. cranberry juice cocktail
½ cup brown sugar, packed
¼ cup granulated sugar, or to taste
1 cinnamon stick, 6 inches
4 whole allspice
5 whole cloves

Place all ingredients in the slow cooker, cover and cook on low heat for 2 to 5 hours. Note: For a little garnish, float a few grapes and cranberries on top of the punch.

EASY CHOCOLATE COFFEE PUNCH

Makes 32 servings

You could not ask for an easier recipe, useful during the holiday rush. An alternative would be to use a coffee flavored ice cream with a drizzle of chocolate syrup or simply add about 1 cup caramel topping.

2 qt. chocolate, cappuccino or ice cream flavor of choice
1 gal. hot coffee
nutmeg or cinnamon for garnish

Place ice cream in slow cooker and pour in hot coffee. Using a whisk, stir until ice cream melts. Cover and cook on low heat for 1 to 4 hours. Sprinkle with nutmeg or cinnamon before serving.

RUSSIAN HOT TODDY

The beauty of this recipe is that the drink mix can be made ahead of time and kept in an airtight container. Then simply add hot water and stir.

3 cups granulated sugar
2 cups orange powdered concentrate drink
1 cup instant tea mix, unsweetened
1 tsp. cinnamon
3/4 tsp. ground cloves
lemon and orange slices for garnish

In a bowl, combine all ingredients and store in an airtight container. Pour 2 quarts of boiling water into the slow cooker and stir in 1 cup of the dry toddy mix. Taste and determine if you wish to add more toddy mix. Cook on low heat for 1 hour before serving. Keep mixture warm for 5 to 6 hours. To make individual cups, stir 2 tbs. toddy mix into one cup of boiling water.

SPICED HOT TEA

Makes 2 quarts

Next time the girls come over for tea, surprise them with this spiced tea. For those sensitive to caffeine, decaffeinated black tea may be substituted. Serve with Almond Cranberry Cake, *page 132,* Banana Nut Cake, *page 122,* Cherry Clafouti, *page 135 or* Pumpkin Date Bread, *page 94.*

2 qt. boiling water
1 six-inch cinnamon stick
one 2½-inch piece peeled fresh ginger,
  cut into ¼-inch slices
1 tsp. coriander seeds
1 tsp. cardamom seeds

1 tsp. whole cloves
¾ tsp. black peppercorns
6 black tea bags
2 cups milk or nut milk
honey to taste

Pour boiling water into the slow cooker and add cinnamon stick, ginger, coriander, cardamom, cloves and peppercorns. Cover and cook on low heat for 2 to 3 hours. Add teabags, milk and honey. Cook on low heat for ½ hour. Remove tea bags, taste and adjust seasonings. Remove floating spices with a strainer before serving. Keep tea warm in cooker.

ROASTED RED PEPPER SAUCE

Servings: 6 as an entrée

This Italian specialty sauce can be used as a dipping sauce for toasted bread rounds, large crackers or vegetables; as an entrée sauce to serve over pasta or rice; or as a sauce to use for pasta casserole dishes like meatless lasagna.

6 extra-large red bell peppers
1 cup chopped onions
2–3 tbs. olive oil
1 ½ tsp. minced garlic
3 tomatoes, seeded and finely chopped,
    or 1 can (1 lb.) tomatoes, drained

3 tbs. chopped fresh basil, or 1 tbs.
    dried
salt to taste
black pepper to taste
⅓ cup chopped fresh parsley

Place bell peppers under broiler, turning frequently until skin is charred black. Place charred peppers in a paper bag for 10 minutes to loosen skin. Remove most of the charred skin with a knife. Do not wash in water or you will lose flavor. Cut peppers in half, remove seeds, cut into strips and cut strips in half. In a skillet on medium-high heat, cook onions in olive oil until onions are translucent. Add garlic and cook for 1 minute. Transfer onion mixture to the slow cooker with remaining ingredients. Cover and cook on low heat for 2 to 3 hours. Remove ⅓ of the mixture, place in a blender and puree until smooth. Return to slow cooker and cook for 1 to 3 hours. Taste and adjust seasonings.

CRANBERRY CHUTNEY

Makes 1 quart

Cranberry chutney has so many uses: serve it as a spread in sandwiches, or as an accompaniment to Mixed Nut Loaf, *page 8,* Carrot Nut Loaf, *page 23, and rice dishes. I like to use Granny Smith, Golden Delicious or Newton apples.*

1 lb. fresh cranberries
1²/₃ cups sugar, or to taste
1 cup raisins
1 cup peeled, chopped apples
1 cup water
1/2 cup chopped onion
1/2 cup finely chopped celery
1 tbs. chopped candied ginger
1 tbs. cinnamon
1/4 tsp. ground cloves
1 pinch ground allspice

Place all ingredients in the slow cooker and stir to combine. Cover and cook on high heat for 2 hours. Remove cover and continue to cook for 1 hour. Taste and adjust seasonings.

RAISIN CHUTNEY

The combination of raisins, apples, onions and spices makes this delicious chutney something special. I like to add this to cream or sour cream and serve over rice. It can also serve as a side dish to lentils or as a sauce to sweeten vegetables.

1 cup golden raisins
1 cup dark raisins
1 cup dried currants
1 cup finely chopped onions
4 cups diced peeled tart apples
1 cup vinegar
1 cup dry white wine or apple cider

$1/2$–$3/4$ cup sugar
1 tbs. diced candied ginger
1 tsp. salt
$1/2$ tsp. allspice
$1/8$ tsp. ground cloves
$1/4$ cup diced green bell peppers
$1/4$ cup diced pimiento

Place all ingredients, except peppers and pimiento, in the slow cooker. Cover and cook on low heat for 4 to 6 hours. Add peppers and pimiento and cook uncovered on high heat for 1 to 2 hours. Taste and adjust seasonings.

TOMATO AND ONION CHUTNEY

Makes 3 cups

This would make a delicious condiment with Greek Eggplant Moussaka, *page 32,* Vegetable Curry, *page 28, or* Cashew and Rice Loaf, *page 22.*

2 tbs. olive oil
1 cup diced yellow onion
1 tsp. minced garlic
5 tomatoes, seeded and diced
1/3 cup raisins
3 tbs. chopped fresh parsley
2 tbs. tomato paste
2 tbs. apple cider vinegar or rice vinegar
2 tbs. honey

1 tbs. minced fresh ginger, or 1 tsp.
   ground
1 tsp. salt
1 tsp. dry mustard
1/2 tsp. dried oregano
1/4 tsp. red pepper flakes
1 qt. water
3/4 lb. pearl onions, unpeeled

In a skillet on medium-high heat, heat olive oil and sauté onions for about 4 to 5 minutes, until soft. Add minced garlic and cook for 1 minute. Transfer to the slow cooker. Add tomatoes, raisins, parsley, tomato paste, apple cider, honey, ginger, salt, mustard, oregano and pepper flakes. In a large saucepan, boil water and drop in pearl onions. Blanch onions for 3 to 4 minutes. Remove from water, cut off root ends and slip onions out of their skins. Add peeled onions to slow cooker. Cover and cook on low heat for 6 to 8 hours.

DESSERTS

BROWN RICE PUDDING

Rice pudding is the ultimate comfort food. Brown rice adds a somewhat chewy texture and nutty flavor to the pudding. As an alternative to raisins, use any other dried fruit or combination of dried fruit. If desired, garnish with sweetened whipped cream or cashew cream.

$2^1/_2$ cups cooked brown rice
$1^1/_2$ cups evaporated milk
$^1/_2$ cup raisins or dried fruit of choice, or more to taste
$^2/_3$ cup brown sugar, or $^1/_2$ cup maple syrup or concentrated fruit sweetener
2 tbs. butter
$^1/_2$ tsp. cinnamon
1 pinch ground cardamom
1 pinch salt
1 pinch ginger

In a bowl, mix all ingredients together and pour into the slow cooker. Cook on high heat for 1 to 2 hours, stirring at least once during the first 30 minutes. Taste and adjust seasonings. Serve either hot or cold.

GINGERED CARROT CAKE

Serve this delicious cake with a dollop of sweetened whipped cream, ice cream, cream cheese frosting or warm bottled caramel sauce. Grated zucchini can be substituted for the carrots, but it should be placed in a clean towel and squeezed to remove excess moisture.

1 cup flour	$1/4$ tsp. ground cloves
1 cup sugar	2 large eggs
1 tsp. salt	$3/4$ cup vegetable oil
1 tsp. baking soda	2 cups grated carrots
1 tsp. cinnamon	$1/2$ cup chopped walnuts or pecans
$3/4$ tsp. allspice	2 cups hot water
$1/2$ tsp. ground ginger	

Sift together flour, sugar, salt, soda, cinnamon, allspice, ginger and cloves. Stir in eggs and oil; stir in carrots and nuts. Pour into a greased, floured 6-cup mold. Cover mold with foil and tie down with string.

Place mold on a trivet in the slow cooker. Pour hot water into slow cooker. Cover and cook on high heat for $2^1/2$ to $3^1/2$ hours, until a knife inserted in the center comes out clean.

DATE PUDDING WITH BUTTERSCOTCH SAUCE
Servings: 6–8

This dessert is a moist, sweet pudding that is steamed in a slow cooker. Serve this pudding warm with a scoop of ice cream and drizzle with butterscotch sauce.

1¾ cups chopped dates
2 cups water
1¾ tsp. baking soda
6 tbs. butter
1 cup sugar
3 large eggs
2 cups flour
½ tsp. ground ginger
½ tsp. baking powder
⅓ tsp. salt
2 cups hot water

SAUCE
¾ cup butter plus 2 tbs.
1⅓ cups brown sugar, packed
1 cup heavy cream
¾ tsp. vanilla extract

In a medium saucepan, cook dates in water uncovered for 5 minutes. Remove pan from heat and stir in baking soda. Cool for 15 minutes.

With a mixer, beat butter and sugar together until light and fluffy. Add eggs one at a time, beating well after adding each egg.

In a small bowl, combine flour, ginger, baking powder and salt. Beat flour mixture into egg mixture, and then gently stir in cooled date mixture. Grease a 2-pound coffee can and layer the bottom with waxed paper. Pour cake mixture into prepared coffee can, cover tightly with foil and tie with string. Place can in the slow cooker and add 2 cups hot water. Cover and cook on high heat for 4 to 4½ hours, until a knife inserted in the center comes out clean. Be sure to check water level and add more water if needed.

To make sauce: Melt butter on medium heat in a small saucepan. Add brown sugar and bring to a boil. Reduce heat and stir in cream. Simmer for about 5 minutes, stirring occasionally. Remove from heat and stir in vanilla. Serve warm sauce over date pudding.

FRUITED TAPIOCA

Slow cookers are ideal for rehydrating dried fruits. Use any combination of dried fruits in this recipe. Serve chilled with a dollop of whipped cream or vanilla ice cream.

1 pkg. (11 oz.) mixed dried fruit
3 cups water
1 cinnamon stick, 6 inches
1 cup white grape juice
$1/3$ cup quick-cooking tapioca
$1/4$ cup sugar
$1/4$ tsp. salt
1 tsp. vanilla extract

Place dried fruit, water and cinnamon stick in the slow cooker, cover and cook on low heat for $2^{1}/_{2}$ hours.

Mix grape juice with tapioca, sugar and salt and allow time for tapioca to soften.

Add tapioca mixture to cooked fruits. Cover and set slow cooker on high heat. Cook for about 10 minutes, until mixture thickens.

Remove from heat and stir in vanilla. Refrigerate until ready to eat.

HOT FUDGE CHERRY CAKE

Servings: 8

In this recipe, water is poured over the batter to create a hot fudge sauce on top of the cake. Try sprinkling this cake with ¹/₂ cup chopped toasted walnuts or pecans. Serve warm with whipped cream or a scoop of vanilla ice cream.

¹/₄ cup butter
3 oz. unsweetened chocolate, divided
1 cup brown sugar, packed, divided
1 cup flour
2 tsp. baking powder
¹/₄ tsp. salt

¹/₃ cup milk
1¹/₄ tsp. vanilla extract
1 can (16 oz.) pitted cherries, drained
1³/₄ cups boiling water
2 cups hot water

In a saucepan on low heat, melt butter and 2 oz. of the chocolate.

Grate remaining chocolate and mix with ¹/₂ cup of the brown sugar.

In a bowl, mix flour, baking powder, salt and remaining brown sugar. Stir in milk, melted chocolate and vanilla until well mixed. Gently stir in cherries.

Butter a baking dish that will fit in your slow cooker. Pour batter into dish and set dish on a trivet in cooker. Sprinkle grated chocolate mixture on top of batter. Pour boiling water over grated chocolate. Tightly cover with foil and tie with string. Add 2 cups hot water around the baking dish. Cover and cook on high heat for 3 to 4 hours.

COFFEE BREAD PUDDING

You can't imagine a better comfort food than this pudding! Toasting the bread cubes will give the bread pudding a wonderful nutty flavor. Serve warm with vanilla ice cream or sweetened whipped cream.

$1\frac{1}{2}$ cups cream or cashew cream
$1\frac{1}{2}$ cups milk
$\frac{2}{3}$–$\frac{3}{4}$ cup gourmet coffee grounds
4 large eggs
$\frac{3}{4}$ cup sugar

1 pinch salt
7 cups toasted 1-inch bread cubes
$\frac{3}{4}$ cup semisweet chocolate chips
$\frac{3}{4}$ cup sliced toasted almonds

In a saucepan on medium-high heat, scald milk (heat until almost boiling). Remove milk from heat and stir in coffee grounds. Steep for 10 minutes; pour through a sieve to remove grounds.

In a bowl, whisk eggs with sugar and salt. Add steeped milk and stir well. Gently stir in bread cubes and chocolate chips and pour into the slow cooker. Cover and cook on low heat for 5 to 6 hours, or on high heat for $1\frac{1}{2}$ to 2 hours.

Sprinkle with toasted nuts and serve warm.

HARVEST CAKE

This is a simple, moist cake loaded with apples, dates and nuts. Serve hot or cold with a dollop of sweetened whipped cream. This would go well at breakfast, brunch or a tea party. If desired, sprinkle top of cake with confectioners' sugar.

4 cups diced apples, peeled if desired
1/2 cup chopped dates
1 cup sugar
1/2 cup flour
2 tsp. baking powder
1 large egg

1 tbs. butter, melted
1 tsp. vanilla extract
3/4 cup chopped toasted walnuts or
    pecans
2 cups hot water

In a large bowl, stir together all ingredients, but do not overbeat. Pour into a greased baking dish that will fit in your slow cooker, cover with foil and tie with string.

Place baking dish on a trivet or rack in the slow cooker with 2 cups hot water. Cover and cook on high heat for 2 1/2 to 3 1/2 hours or until a knife inserted in the center comes out clean.

RASPBERRY PEACH CRISP

This recipe is reminiscent of peach melba with an oat crumble topping. For an alternative, use blackberries, Marionberries or loganberries in place of raspberries. Serve with ice cream or sweetened whipped cream.

1 pkg. (10 oz.) frozen or fresh raspberries
1/2 cup sugar
3 tbs. cornstarch
4 cups sliced peaches, fresh or canned
1 cup rolled oats
3/4 cup flour
3/4 cup brown sugar, packed
1/2 tsp. cinnamon
1/4 tsp. salt
1/2 cup butter

Defrost berries and place in a saucepan with sugar and cornstarch. Cook on medium heat for 4 to 5 minutes, until sauce becomes translucent. If you prefer a seedless sauce, press the sauce through a sieve with the back of a spoon.

Pour sauce into the slow cooker and stir in peaches.

Spread oats on a baking sheet and place under the broiler until oats turn light brown. Be very careful not to burn oats. Allow oats to cool before mixing with butter.

In a bowl, combine flour, brown sugar, cinnamon and salt. Cut butter into flour mixture with a pastry blender or two knives until butter pieces are about the size of peas. Stir in cooled, toasted oatmeal and spread mixture on top of peaches to within $1/2$-inch of edge of cooker. This will allow moisture to escape and prevent crisp from becoming too soggy.

Cover and cook on high heat for $1 1/2$ hours.

MISSISSIPPI MUD CAKE

This rich, moist chocolate cake is loaded with nuts and coconut. A recipe for fudge frosting is included, but consider using a chocolate cream cheese frosting— or eliminate the frosting and serve with chocolate ice cream.

³/₄ cup butter
2 cups sugar
4 large eggs
1 tsp. vanilla extract
1 ¹/₂ cups flour
²/₃ cup cocoa powder

1 ¹/₂ cups chopped toasted walnuts or
   pecans
1 cup shredded coconut
1 jar (7 oz.) marshmallow creme
2 cups hot water

With a mixer, cream butter and sugar together until light and fluffy. Add eggs and vanilla and mix well. Mix flour and cocoa powder together and beat into butter mixture. Stir in nuts and coconut.

Pour mixture into a greased 1 ¹/₂-quart baking dish, cover dish with foil and tie with string. Place dish on a trivet or rack in the slow cooker and pour in 2 cups hot water.

Cover and cook on high heat for 3 to 4 hours, or until a knife inserted in the center comes out clean. Remove baking dish from cooker and immediately spread cake with marshmallow creme. When cool, spread with frosting.

CHOCOLATE FROSTING

1/2 cup butter
4 cups sifted confectioners' sugar
1 tsp. vanilla extract
1/2 cup cocoa powder
1/2 cup evaporated milk
1 pinch salt

With a mixer, blend all ingredients together until smooth. Taste and add more cocoa powder and a little more milk for a stronger chocolate flavor if desired.

BANANA NUT CAKE

Whenever you have leftover bananas, peel, freeze them and use them for bread and cake recipes. Banana extract is usually found in health food stores or large supermarkets, but if it is not readily available, use vanilla extract.

$^1/_2$ cup butter
1$^1/_2$ cups sugar
2 large eggs, beaten
2 cups flour
2 tsp. baking powder
1 pinch salt
$^1/_2$ cup sour milk, buttermilk or milk
1 tsp. baking soda
3 medium bananas, mashed
1 tsp. banana or vanilla extract
1 cup chopped toasted walnuts
2 cups hot water

With a mixer, cream butter and sugar together and beat in eggs.

Mix flour, baking powder and salt together and add flour mixture and sour milk to creamed butter mixture.

Mix baking soda with mashed banana and banana extract and blend into creamed butter mixture. Stir in chopped nuts and pour into a buttered 1½-quart baking dish. Cover dish with foil and tie with string. Place baking dish on a trivet or rack in the slow cooker and pour in 2 cups hot water. Cover and cook on high heat for 2½ to 3½ hours, until a knife inserted in the center comes out clean.

Allow cake to cool before spreading with frosting.

CREAM CHEESE FROSTING

¼ cup butter, softened
6 oz. cream cheese, softened
2 cups sifted confectioners' sugar
1 tsp. banana or vanilla extract

With a mixer, blend all ingredients together until smooth.

STEAMED CHOCOLATE PUDDING

Servings: 6

Steamed puddings are ideal for slow cookers. Serve this chocolate pudding with or without toasted nuts and smothered in bottled fudge sauce, caramel sauce or vanilla ice cream.

1/4 cup butter, softened, divided
3/4 cup sugar, plus 1 tbs. sugar for dusting
2 large eggs, separated
1/3 cup chocolate milk
2 tbs. chocolate liqueur, Grand Marnier liqueur or apple
 juice
3/4 cup flour
2 tsp. baking powder
1/4 cup unsweetened cocoa
2 tbs. unseasoned dry breadcrumbs
3/4 cup chopped toasted walnuts or pecans,
 optional
2 cups hot water

Use 1 tbs. of the butter to grease a 1-pound coffee can and dust with 1 tbs. sugar. With a mixer, beat together remaining butter and sugar until mixture is fluffy. Add egg yolks and beat until smooth.

Mix together chocolate milk and liqueur of choice.

In a small bowl, combine flour, baking powder, cocoa and breadcrumbs. Add flour mixture and milk mixture to butter mixture. Stir in walnuts. With a mixer, beat egg whites together until stiff peaks form. Fold egg whites into chocolate mixture.

Pour batter into prepared can, cover with foil and tie with string. Place can on a trivet or rack in the slow cooker and add 2 cups hot water. Cover and cook on high heat for 3½ hours, until a wooden skewer inserted in the center comes out clean.

Remove coffee can from slow cooker and let stand for 5 minutes. Open bottom with can opener and push pudding through can. Serve warm.

CITRUS STEAMED PUDDING

Servings: 6

If you prefer not to use liqueur in this recipe, simply substitute orange juice. Serve with bottled lemon or lime curd, warmed orange marmalade, orange-flavored frosting or ice cream.

1 tbs. butter
1 tbs. granulated sugar for dusting
$\frac{1}{2}$ cup finely chopped candied lemon peel
$\frac{1}{4}$ cup orange curaçao, Tía Maria, or Grand Marnier liqueur
1 tbs. grated orange peel
1 cup flour
2 tsp. baking powder
$\frac{1}{4}$ cup dried unseasoned breadcrumbs
$\frac{1}{4}$ cup butter
$\frac{2}{3}$ cup sugar
2 large eggs
$\frac{1}{4}$ cup orange juice
2 cups hot water

Grease a 1-pound coffee can with butter and dust sides and bottom with sugar.

In a small bowl, combine candied lemon peel, orange liqueur and grated orange peel.

In a bowl, mix together flour, baking powder and breadcrumbs.

With a mixer, beat together butter and sugar until fluffy. Add eggs and mix well. Add flour mixture and orange juice to butter mixture, blending well. Add lemon peel mixture and stir to combine.

Pour batter into prepared coffee can. Cover with foil and tie with string. Place can on a trivet or rack in the slow cooker, add 2 cups hot water, cover and cook on high heat for 3 to 4 hours, until a wooden skewer inserted in the center comes out clean.

Remove can from slow cooker and cool for 5 minutes. Open bottom of can with a can opener and push pudding through can. Serve warm.

HAZELNUT CAKE

Toasting hazelnuts really brings out their flavor. For a change, you might want to add ¹/₂ cup coconut. Serve warm with chocolate sauce, fudge sauce, coffee-flavored frosting or sweetened whipped cream.

³/₄ cup chopped hazelnuts
³/₄ cup brown sugar, packed
¹/₂ cup vegetable oil
¹/₂ cup strong espresso coffee, cooled to room temperature
2 tbs. hazelnut or coffee liqueur
4 large eggs, separated
1¹/₂ cups flour
2 tsp. cinnamon
¹/₂ tsp. salt
1 pinch nutmeg
1 pinch ground allspice
2 cups hot water

Place chopped hazelnuts on a cookie sheet, set under a broiler and toast nuts to a light brown color. Watch nuts carefully to avoid burning.

With a mixer, blend together toasted hazelnuts, brown sugar, oil, coffee and liqueur. Beat in egg yolks until well mixed.

In a small bowl, mix together flour, cinnamon, salt, nutmeg and allspice. Add to nut mixture, stirring well to combine.

With a mixer, beat egg whites to soft peaks and gently fold into nut mixture.

Grease a steam pudding pan or coffee can, pour in batter, cover with foil and tie with string. Place a trivet or rack in the slow cooker. Add 2 cups hot water, cover and cook on high heat for $2\frac{1}{2}$ to $3\frac{1}{2}$ hours, until a wooden skewer inserted in the center comes out clean.

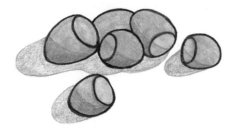

CAROB CHEESECAKE

This is a multi-layered cheesecake consisting of a graham cracker crust, a dark carob layer, a yogurt layer and finally a carob sauce on top. Carob powder can be found in health food stores and large supermarkets.

2½ cups graham cracker crumbs
1 tsp. cinnamon
½ cup sugar
⅔ cup butter, melted
¼ cup ground toasted almonds
½ cup milk
5½ tbs. arrowroot powder, divided
3 tbs. vanilla extract, divided
⅔ cup pure maple syrup, divided

⅔ cup carob powder, divided
8 oz. cream cheese
3 cups yogurt, drained through a sieve
  for 4 hours, or sour cream
3 tbs. butter
3 tbs. honey
¼–½ cup milk for thinning, optional
½ cup chopped toasted almonds or
  cashews

Heat oven to 375.° In a bowl, combine graham cracker crumbs, cinnamon, sugar, melted butter and ground almonds. Press into a greased 9-inch springform pan or other pan that will fit in your slow cooker. Bake for 15 to 20 minutes, until crust is browned. Cool.

With a mixer, blend together milk, 4 tbs. of the arrowroot, 1 tbs. of the vanilla, $1/2$ of the maple syrup, $1/2$ of the carob powder and cream cheese. Pour over cooled crust and cover with foil. Place pan directly in the slow cooker, cover and cook on high heat for $1 1/2$ to 2 hours.

With a food processor or blender, cream together drained yogurt, remaining vanilla and remaining maple syrup and pour over partially cooked cheesecake. Cover with foil and bake for 1 to $1 1/2$ hours, until a knife inserted in the center comes out clean.

In a blender container or food processor workbowl, blend together butter, honey, remaining carob powder and remaining arrowroot until smooth. If you prefer a thinner sauce, add a little milk and stir until smooth. Spread sauce over top of cooled cake. Refrigerate until ready to serve. Sprinkle with nuts before serving.

ALMOND CRANBERRY CAKE

Servings: 8

This wonderful, moist cake can be served as a breakfast coffeecake or for tea. For a change, try substituting almond extract for vanilla. For a nice accompaniment, serve with cranberry butter: mix jellied cranberry sauce with softened butter to taste. For garnish, sprinkle with confectioners' sugar.

2 cups coarsely chopped fresh
   cranberries
2/3 cup brown sugar, packed
3/4 cup chopped toasted almonds
2 tsp. cinnamon
1/4 tsp. nutmeg
1/8 tsp. ground allspice
1/2 cup butter
1 cup sugar

1 tsp. vanilla extract
1 cup sour cream
2 large eggs, beaten
2 cups flour
1 tsp. baking powder
1 tsp. baking soda
1/4 tsp. salt
confectioners' sugar for sprinkling

In a bowl, combine cranberries, brown sugar, almonds, cinnamon, nutmeg and allspice.

With a mixer, beat together butter and sugar until light and fluffy. Add vanilla, sour cream and eggs and beat until creamy. Sift flour, baking powder, baking soda and salt and stir into butter mixture, blending until just combined.

Butter a baking dish that will fit in your slow cooker. Pour ½ of the batter into dish and sprinkle ½ of the cranberry mixture over batter. Repeat with remaining batter and cranberry mixture.

Cover baking dish with foil and tie with string. Place dish in slow cooker, cover and cook on high heat for 2 to 3 hours, until a knife inserted in the center comes out clean. Cool and sprinkle with confectioners' sugar.

CARAWAY SEED TEA CAKE

This simple cake has the unique flavor of caraway and requires no icing. Serve thinly sliced, spread with butter, flavored butter or cream cheese.

1 cup butter
1 cup sugar
5 large eggs
1 tsp. vanilla extract
2 cups flour

1 tsp. baking powder
1/2 tsp. salt
2 tbs. caraway seeds
2 cups hot water

With a mixer, cream together butter and sugar until fluffy. Beat in eggs, one at a time, beating well after each addition. Add vanilla, flour, baking powder, salt and caraway seeds.

Pour mixture into a buttered round baking dish. Cover with foil and tie with string. Place dish on a trivet or rack in the slow cooker and add 2 cups hot water. Cover and cook on high heat for 2 to 3 hours, until a knife inserted in the center comes out clean. Remove from cooker and let stand for 10 minutes before serving.

CHERRY CLAFOUTI

A clafouti is a cake with a pudding texture, loaded with fruit and eggs and flavored with brandy. Try plums, apricots or even peaches in place of cherries.

1 cup flour, sifted
4 large eggs, beaten
3 tbs. superfine sugar
1 pinch salt
2½ cups milk
1 lb. sweet pitted cherries, fresh or
  canned, drained

2–3 tbs. brandy, amaretto or cherry
  brandy
2 tbs. confectioners' sugar or superfine
  sugar for sprinkling
2 cups hot water

Place flour in a bowl and make a well in the center. Add eggs, sugar and salt and slowly incorporate mixture into flour. Add milk and stir until smooth.

Butter a 4-cup baking dish or soufflé dish and place ½ of the batter in dish. Spoon cherries over batter, spoon remaining batter on top of cherries and drizzle brandy on top.

Cover baking dish with foil and tie with string. Set dish on a trivet or rack in the slow cooker and add 2 cups hot water. Cover and cook on high heat for 2 to 3 hours. Sprinkle with confectioners' sugar before serving.

APPENDIX:
Substitutions for Meat and Dairy Products

SUGGESTED SUBSTITUTIONS

Butter   Use an equivalent amount of nut butter, avocado or olive oil

Use up to ¼ cup applesauce or pureed prunes (do not overbeat)

Use 2 parts olive oil to 1 part light miso in equivalent measure

Use soy margarine in equivalent measure

Use 80% amount oil in place of butter in baking (you may need to increase the flour slightly)

Buttermilk   Use equivalent amounts almond milk or cashew milk (add 1 tsp. vinegar or lemon juice per cup milk required)

Cheese
   cheddar   Use equivalent amount cheddar-style soy or millet cheese

   cottage   Use equivalent amount *Sour Cream Substitute (Tofu),* page 142 or *Mock Cream Cheese,* page 149

   cream cheese   Use equivalent amount *Mock Cream Cheese,* page 149, or *Almond Cream Mayonnaise Substitute,* page 148

   Monterey Jack   Use equivalent amount Monterey Jack-style soy or millet cheese

   mozzarella   Use equivalent amount mozzarella-style soy or millet cheese

jalapeño pepper	Use equivalent amount jalapeño-style soy or millet cheese
ricotta	Use equivalent amount *Ricotta Substitute,* page 141
Chocolate	For every 1-ounce square, use 3 tbs. carob powder and 1 tbs. vegetable oil
Cocoa	Use equivalent amount carob powder
Cream	Use equivalent amount *Cashew Cream,* page 146, or for every ½ cup cream use 2 tbs. tahini mixed with ½ cup water
Eggs	
baking	Use commercially available egg replacer product, according to package instructions
	Use ½ ripe banana for each egg required
	Use ¼ cup tofu for each egg required
	Use 1 tbs. powdered soy lecithin with 1 tbs. water for each egg required
	Use ¼ cup reconstituted, dried, pureed apricots or prunes for each egg required
in salads	Use diced or crumbled firm tofu
scrambled	Use tofu and tofu scrambler seasoning (see instructions on box)

Gelatin	Use 1 tbs. "granulated" agar-agar to $3\frac{1}{2}$ cups water
	Use 2 tbs. "flaked" agar-agar to $3\frac{1}{2}$ cups water
Honey	Use $1\frac{1}{4}$ cups brown rice syrup or concentrated for each cup honey required
	Use equivalent amount barley malt syrup or sorghum molasses
	Use $\frac{3}{4}$ cup maple syrup for each cup honey required
Lard	For every cup required use 1 cup soy margarine or $\frac{3}{4}$ cup vegetable oil
Milk	Use equivalent amount almond milk, cashew milk or soy milk
Molasses (blackstrap)	Use equivalent amount barley malt syrup, sorghum molasses, or brown rice syrup
Salt (processed)	Use herb blends, salt-free seasoning or ground rock salt to taste
	Use powdered kelp, dulse or miso to taste
	Use tamari or umeboshi plum paste to taste
Sour cream	Use equivalent amount soft tofu with $\frac{1}{2}$ tsp. lemon juice per cup required, or use *Sour Cream Substitute,* page 142
Soy sauce	Use $\frac{1}{2}$ the amount low sodium tamari or Braggs liquid aminos (a low-fat, low-sodium health-food product, similar to soy sauce)

Sugar, brown	Use ³/₄ cup maple syrup or honey for every cup brown sugar required. If using maple syrup, reduce liquid by 2 tbs. for every cup sweetener. If using honey, reduce liquid by ¹/₂ cup for every cup of sweetener, reduce oven temperature by 25° and add ¹/₂ tsp. baking soda
	Use ²/₃ to 1 cup Sucanat (a natural sugar product made from dried cane juice granules) for each cup sugar required
Sugar, white	Use equivalent amount date sugar
	Use ³/₄ cup maple syrup for each cup sugar required and reduce other liquids by 2 tbs. for each cup maple syrup used
	Use ³/₄ cup honey for each cup sugar required and reduce other liquids by ¹/₂ cup for each cup honey used; reduce oven temperature by 25° and add ¹/₂ tsp. baking soda
	Use equivalent amount sorghum molasses and reduce other liquids by ¹/₄ cup for each cup molasses used; add ¹/₂ tsp. baking soda per 1 cup molasses used
	Use ²/₃ to 1 cup Fruit Source (dried white grape juice) or Sucanat for each cup sugar required.
Yogurt	Use equivalent amount soft tofu

RICOTTA SUBSTITUTE

This recipe is great for dishes like lasagna or filled crepes. The nutmeg is an optional ingredient but adds a little extra flavor that goes well with vegetables.

1 lb. firm tofu
$\frac{1}{3}$ cup olive oil
$\frac{1}{2}$ tsp. salt or seasoned salt
1 pinch nutmeg, optional

Place $\frac{3}{4}$ lb. of the tofu in a blender container with olive oil and salt. Blend until smooth. Taste and add nutmeg and additional salt if desired. To create some texture, mash remaining $\frac{1}{4}$ lb. tofu with a fork and stir into smooth tofu mixture.

APPENDIX: SUBSTITUTIONS FOR MEAT AND DAIRY PRODUCTS   141

SOUR CREAM SUBSTITUTE (TOFU)

Makes 2–2½ cups

This is a tangy tofu substitute that can be used in any recipe requiring sour cream. It is especially suitable as a topping for potatoes.

6 oz. firm silken tofu
1 tbs. vegetable oil
2 tbs. lemon juice
1 tbs. tahini (sesame paste)
2 tsp. rice vinegar
salt to taste

Place tofu in a steamer and cook for 2 minutes. Transfer steamed tofu to a blender container with remaining ingredients. Blend until smooth. Taste and adjust seasonings.

SOUR CREAM SUBSTITUTE (SUNFLOWER SEED)

This is a great sour cream alternative for people who are allergic to tofu or avoid dairy products. Consider blending tomatoes or avocados with this recipe to make a great salad dressing.

²/₃ cup sunflower seeds
²/₃–³/₄ cup water
2–3 tbs. fresh lemon juice
¹/₂ tsp. salt
¹/₂ tsp. onion powder
¹/₄ tsp. garlic powder

Place all ingredients in a blender container, using smaller quantities of water and lemon juice to start. Blend until smooth. Taste and add more water if you prefer a thinner mixture or more lemon juice for a tangier mixture. Adjust seasonings to your personal taste. Keep in a covered container in the refrigerator.

RICE MILK

Rice milk is a good alternative to dairy products. To make carob rice milk add 3 tbs. carob powder and ½ tsp. vanilla extract to 1 quart rice milk and sweeten to taste.

1 cup cooked brown rice
1¼ cups boiling water
3 tbs. ground raw cashews or almonds
1–2 tsp. honey
¼ tsp. salt
1½ cups cold water

Place all ingredients except cold water in a blender container and blend until creamy. Add cold water and pour through a sieve. Cover and refrigerate until ready to use.

NUT MILKS

Use nut milks measure for measure as substitutes for dairy milk. Nut milks have a tendency to break down when boiled. Add them at the end of cooking and heat gently before serving. Store nut milks covered in the refrigerator for 4 or 5 days. Cashew milk is generally used as a substitute for milk or cream in cooking, while almond milk is better as a beverage. The maple syrup is an optional ingredient. I do use sweeteners when serving nut milk as a beverage.

1 cup blanched almonds or cashews
1 qt. water
2 tbs. maple syrup, brown rice syrup or concentrated fruit sweetener

With a blender, grind nuts into a fine powder. Add 2 cups of the water and blend for 2 minutes, until smooth. Slowly pour remaining 2 cups water into blender container with the motor running. Blend for an additional 2 minutes. Taste and add sweetener if desired. Strain mixture through several layers of cheesecloth to remove nut residue. Pour strained mixture into a sealed jar and refrigerate until ready to serve.

CREAM SUBSTITUTE (CASHEW CREAM)

Makes 1½ cups

Use cashew cream measure for measure for recipes requiring cream. Do not heat to boiling or the cream will break.

½ cup raw cashews
1½ cups water
2 tsp. maple syrup, brown rice syrup or concentrated fruit sweetener

Place all ingredients in a blender container and process on high for about 3 minutes, until mixture is smooth. If you wish a thinner mixture, simply add a little more water.

MAYONNAISE SUBSTITUTE (SESAME CREAM) Makes 2½ cups

This savory recipe is a great substitute for mayonnaise. Use this recipe for salad dressings, as a spread for grain burgers or sandwiches and as a dip for vegetables.

1 cup tahini (sesame paste)
1 tsp. minced garlic
½ cup water, or more if mixture is thick
2 tsp. salt
⅔ cup lemon juice,or more to taste

Place tahini, garlic, water and salt in a blender container and process on high until mixture makes a paste. Add lemon juice and more water if you wish a thinner paste. Taste and adjust seasonings. Place in a covered container and refrigerate until ready to use.

MAYONNAISE SUBSTITUTE (ALMOND CREAM)

Makes 1¾ cups

This is another great substitute for mayonnaise. It is very important that you add the oil slowly so the mixture will emulsify properly. Adding the oil too quickly can cause the mixture to break and take on a curdled appearance.

½ cup blanched almonds
½ cup almond milk, soy milk or water, divided
1 tbs. protein powder (soy or rice based)
1 tsp. nutritional yeast

1 pinch garlic powder
¾ tsp. ground rock salt or seasoning salt, or to taste
1 cup vegetable oil
3 tbs. lemon juice
1 scant tsp. apple cider vinegar

Grind almonds with a food processor or blender until nuts are turned to powder. Add ¼ cup of the almond milk, protein powder, yeast, garlic and salt. Process until smooth. Add remaining almond milk and process until smooth. With food processor or blender running, very slowly pour oil into almond mixture until mixture thickens and emulsifies. Add lemon juice and vinegar and mix well. Taste and adjust seasonings. Add a little more water or oil if you desire a thinner mixture. Cover and refrigerate until ready to use. Mixture will keep for about 12 days.

MOCK CREAM CHEESE

This recipe contains only 84 calories compared to 189 calories per cup of cream cheese. Use this as a topping for desserts or vegetables or as a substitute for cream cheese in recipes.

8 oz. soft tofu
1 tbs. maple syrup
1 pinch nutmeg

Mix all ingredients together until smooth. Refrigerate until ready to use.

INDEX

C

I
Italian eggplant and beans 30

J
Jambalaya 36

L
Lasagna 6
Lentil soup with Swiss cheese 56
Lentils with almonds and raisins
 11

M
Macaroni and cashew cheese 42
Many bean chili 14
Mayonnaise substitute (almond
 cream) 148
Mayonnaise substitute (sesame
 cream) 147
Meat substitutions, see Appendix
 137–141
Mexican bean pot 24
Milk, nut 145
Milk, rice 144
Millet cereal, fruited 89
Mississippi mud cake 120
Moussaka, Greek eggplant 32
Mud cake, Mississippi 120

Mush, date cornmeal 87
Mushroom and Parmesan rice 31
Mushroom and tomato rice 73

N
Nacho salad, black bean 41
Navy bean soup 45
Nut loaf, mixed 8
Nut milks 145
Nut(s)
    almond cranberry cake 132
    and banana cake 122
    and carrot loaf 23
    cashew and rice loaf 22
    with cumin rice 71
    hazelnut cake 128
    -stuffed onions 82
    and zucchini bread 96

O
Onion(s)
    bisque 63
    brown sugar-glazed 78
    and fruit with red cabbage 69
    gravy 9
    nut-stuffed 82
    rosemary creamed 75
    soup, French 50

and tomato chutney 108
and turnip casserole 77
Orange and carrot chilled soup 49

P
Parmesan and mushroom rice 31
Parmesan eggplant casserole 12
Parsnip and squash soup 47
Pasta, see macaroni and cashew
    cheese 42
Pasta, see lasagna 6
Peach raspberry crisp 118
Pepper, roasted red sauce 105
Picadillo sweet beans 18
Pie, chili corn 26
Pilaf, bulgur with garbanzo beans
    21
Pineapple carrots, glazed 76
Potato(es)
    and beet borscht 44
    easy scalloped 68
    peel broth 53
    Roquefort 80
    and rutabaga casserole 19
    in spaghetti sauce 65
    spinach soup 57
Provençal vegetable soup 54

Serve Creative, Easy, Nutritious Meals with nitty gritty® Cookbooks

1 or 2, Cooking for
100 Dynamite Desserts
9 x 13 Pan Cookbook
Bagels, Best
Barbecue Cookbook
Beer and Good Food
Big Book of Bread Machine Recipes
Big Book of Kitchen Appliance Recipes
Big Book of Snacks and Appetizers
Blender Drinks
Bread Baking
Bread Machine
Bread Machine II
Bread Machine III
Bread Machine V
Bread Machine VI
Bread Machine, Entrees
Burger Bible
Cappuccino/Espresso
Casseroles
Chicken, Unbeatable
Chile Peppers
Clay, Cooking in

Coffee and Tea
Convection Oven
Cook-Ahead Cookbook
Crockery Pot, Extra-Special
Deep Fryer
Dehydrator Cookbook
Edible Gifts
Edible Pockets
Fabulous Fiber Cookery
Fondue and Hot Dips
Fondue, New International
Freezer, 'Fridge, Pantry
Garlic Cookbook
Grains, Cooking with
Healthy Cooking on Run
Ice Cream Maker
Indoor Grill, Cooking on
Italian Recipes, Quick and Easy
Juicer Book II
Kids, Cooking with Your
Kids, Healthy Snacks for
Loaf Pan, Recipes for
Low-Carb Recipes

Lowfat American
No Salt No Sugar No Fat (REVISED)
Party Foods/Appetizers
Pasta Machine Cookbook
Pasta, Quick and Easy
Pinch of Time
Pizza, Best
Porcelain, Cooking in
Pressure Cooker, Recipes (REVISED)
Rice Cooker
Rotisserie Oven Cooking
Sandwich Maker
Simple Substitutions
Skillet, Sensational
Slow Cooking
Slow Cooker, Vegetarian
Soups and Stews
Soy & Tofu Recipes
Tapas Fantásticas
Toaster Oven Cookbook
Waffles & Pizzelles
Wedding Catering Cookbook
Wraps and Roll-Ups (REVISED)

For a free catalog, call: Bristol Publishing Enterprises
(800) 346-4889
www.bristolpublishing.com